The Psychologically Responsive Leader

Also by this author

My Anxiety Handbook
Getting Back on Track
Sue Knowles, Bridie Gallagher and Phoebe McEwen
Illustrated by Emmeline Pidgen
ISBN 978 1 78592 440 8
eISBN 978 1 78450 813 5
The Handbooks Series

of related interest

A Treasure Box for Creating Trauma-Informed Organizations
A Ready-to-Use Resource for Trauma, Adversity, and Culturally
Informed, Infused and Responsive Systems
Dr. Karen Treisman
ISBN 978 1 78775 312 9
eISBN 978 1 83997 188 4
The Therapeutic Treasures Collection

The Neurodiverse Workplace
An Employer's Guide to Managing and Working with
Neurodivergent Employees, Clients and Customers
Victoria Honeybourne
ISBN 978 1 78775 033 3
eISBN 978 1 78775 034 0

Critical Supervision for the Human Services
A Social Model to Promote Learning and Value-Based Practice
Carolyn Noble, Mel Gray and Lou Johnston
ISBN 978 1 84905 589 5
eISBN 978 1 78450 043 6

Yoga as Self-Care for Healthcare Practitioners
Cultivating Resilience, Compassion, and Empathy
Aggie Stewart
Foreword by John Kepner
ISBN 978 1 84819 396 3
eISBN 978 0 85701 353 8

The Psychologically Responsive Leader

*The EVOLVING framework for health,
social care and education professionals*

SUE KNOWLES
and GILL I'ANSON

Foreword by Dr Sandra Bloom

Jessica Kingsley Publishers
London and Philadelphia

First published in Great Britain in 2025 by Jessica Kingsley Publishers
An imprint of John Murray Press

1

A CIP catalogue record for this title is available from the
British Library and the Library of Congress.

ISBN 978 1 80501 236 8
eISBN 978 1 80501 237 5

Printed and bound in the United Kingdom by CPI Group (UK) Ltd, Croydon CR0 4YY

Jessica Kingsley Publishers' policy is to use papers that are natural,
renewable and recyclable products and made from wood grown in
sustainable forests. The logging and manufacturing processes are expected
to conform to the environmental regulations of the country of origin.

Jessica Kingsley Publishers
Carmelite House
50 Victoria Embankment
London EC4Y 0DZ

www.jkp.com

John Murray Press
Part of Hodder & Stoughton Limited
An Hachette UK Company

The authorised representative in the EEA is Hachette Ireland,
8 Castlecourt Centre, Dublin 15, D15 XTP3, Ireland (email: info@hbgi.ie)

Acknowledgements

Gill would like to thank Sue, who inspires and challenges her to push herself both in her leadership and as an individual. Gill would also like to thank her family members and her many 'can do' friends who constantly show emotional and physical courage in their leadership of their families, their friends and in their work. A special mention to her friend Cath Harding, who is an amazing leader in so many ways. Lastly to Jonny and her children Finn, Jude and Rowan, who provide the biggest purpose in her life, and Rudi the Labradoodle, for always greeting her with love and joy.

Sue would first like to thank Gill, who has been by her side throughout the past few years of her leadership journey, providing support, challenge and lots of fun. She is also thankful to her husband Ben, who has put up with lots of distracted discussions while she is typing up 'book stuff', and who has resisted rolling his eyes each time she has said that she is not writing any more books. Her sons Tom and Toby, for just being them. And her friends Ginny Koppenhol and Rach Lancaster, who are two of her biggest supporters, encouragers and generally inspirational beings.

A big thank you to our draft readers Jeanie McIntee and Dave l'Anson, for their thorough and valued reflections.

Our thanks to all the people who have contributed through discussions, reflections and debates, and by sharing their best practice examples. To Andy Rogers, who has supported, and encouraged, our journey setting up the Centre for Psychologically Responsive

Leadership.[1] We have also learned so much from the many leaders with whom we have worked closely over the years, including those who have been through our EVOLVING leadership course.

We are very grateful to everyone who has shared their thoughts and experiences with us, and who have been generous in giving us their time to contribute to our podcast.

Finally, to our team at Jessica Kingsley Publishers, particularly Amy Lankester-Owen, for believing in us and our ideas.

---

[1] See https://cmcafs.com/evolving-leadership

Contents

Foreword

Dr Sandra Bloom, MD, founder of Creating Presence™,
Associate Professor, Health Management & Policy, Dornsife
School of Public Health, Drexel University, Philadelphia, USA

My first leadership experience was offered to me when I was invited to turn a medical-surgical floor in a small, community-based hospital, located about 50 miles from Philadelphia, into an open, voluntary psychiatric unit for adolescents and adults. I was only a year out of my residency, and as a brand-new start-up medical director, I had absolutely *zero* leadership training or preparation other than mirroring the model of my mentor, Dr Roy Stern. Roy's family had escaped Germany and had immigrated to America to escape the Holocaust. He was psychoanalytically trained, had a caustic sense of humour, little tolerance for stupidity, and was kind and protective of both the patients and the nursing staff.

I trained in an era when social psychiatry still mattered, but in America, the gradual deterioration in psychiatric services secondary to the emphasis on behaviourism and profitability had already begun, and I watched as Roy courageously upheld the basic tenets of good care of the patients and of the staff by repeatedly putting his own integrity on the line with hospital administrators, fighting to maintain the open door of our programme, and the necessary funding for qualified staff. I didn't know it at the time, but he was setting a standard of institutional courage that would be with me for a lifetime.

This is not an unusual story for most people who assume leadership positions in the social services world – nothing to go on except what we have seen in people who have led us. Laurence J. Peter, in his book *The Peter Principle*, observed that people in a hierarchy tend to keep being promoted based on their success in previous jobs until they reach a level at which they are no longer competent. This may be the result of the inabilities of the person, but it is more likely because the person has not yet acquired the necessary leadership skills, largely because they do not even know what those skills are – they are just expected to exercise them, and must then confront repeated failure when they do not do so.

As an approach it is a bit like taking a young child to the beach and having one parent or caregiver say to another, 'Let's just throw them in the water and see if they sink or swim.' No responsible parent or caregiver would do that, and yet that is precisely what we frequently do to young and unseasoned professionals, and then punish them when the decisions they make are not the best. This shouldn't really come as a surprise to anyone since so little attention has been paid to actually preparing people for what they are going to encounter on the job. Even though I had extensive experience by the time I was in a leadership position, it was experience that had exposed me far more to being led than to actually leading!

That is why this book is to be treasured by anyone who is even considering assuming a position of leading other people. By scouring the literature, the web and their own podcasts for basic knowledge, tips and reflections on what it means to be in a leadership position, and to *evolve* in that position, the two authors, Gill l'Anson and Sue Knowles, have done their homework for the reader. In each chapter they highlight theory and definitions around a relevant organizational issue, then move on to practical things you, as a leader, can do to hone your skills, outlining concrete steps you can take, and examples of how this works in a wide variety of settings – a rugby team, a school or university, a law firm, the NHS or a large corporation, for example.

There are many tasks that you may have come to believe characterize what it means to be a leader. But many of those tasks you can distribute among other qualified people to form your own team. As a leader, you must focus on creating and maintaining – and often healing – a safe and supportive culture within which every individual's autonomy, competence and purpose can be actualized. This can only come about through the manifestation of your own integrity, trustworthiness and interpersonal skills. I am grateful for the contribution the authors are making. When I read this book, I only wished that I had been offered such a book when I was first taking on a leadership role, instead of needing to learn it all the hard way.

Preface

After many years working as clinical psychologists in and with health, mental health, social care, secure care, education and legal services, we set up the Centre for Psychologically Responsive Leadership. We became interested in what we term 'psychologically responsive leadership' from our own experiences of leadership, both providing and receiving, and our work within Changing Minds Child and Family Services (CMCAFS). Our work involves supporting organizations in health, education and social care to use the available psychological knowledge, theory and research to help their teams and clients to thrive. We were aware that providing good psychological knowledge at ground level, for working with clients, was limited in its usefulness without such knowledge also being implemented throughout all levels of the organization. We were supporting managers and leaders to develop their psychological understanding, skills and knowledge, and felt that this was where we could have a useful impact on organizations and systems whose purpose it is to support, care for, protect and develop people, which is why we wrote this book.

Introduction

Leadership is a challenging role. Being a good leader is even more challenging. A wealth of leadership books and courses are available, which all outline a number of qualities, skills and expertise that you *should* bring to your role to be successful – which, for many leaders, can feel overwhelming. Most leaders we have worked with feel 'exposed' at times, have doubts about their own skills and experience, and are afraid of not being 'good enough' or failing to meet others' expectations. Although this self-doubt is quite normal, they often feel isolated and may therefore not be aware that others feel similarly, which can lead to feelings of being an 'imposter' or fears of being 'found out'. These fears may be exacerbated when the person has been promoted quickly into a leadership position, without much opportunity for support, development or reflection – a common occurrence within health, social care and education. In addition, a change of position often happens within a crisis. At these times leaders may find themselves picking up more responsibility, needing to steer their team through a particularly difficult time or significant organizational change. They may therefore be trying to 'find their feet' within a leadership position as well as taking on increasing levels of responsibility or demand without having the opportunity to reflect on their own development and without the support they may need to become the type of leader that they want to be.

Over the past few decades, it has been recognized that an authoritarian leadership style ('big chief') only goes so far, and there is a need for leaders to be more empowering, compassionate and understanding of the needs and challenges of the people they lead. The skills, qualities and knowledge required for leadership have shifted, and now focus predominantly on how leaders can build healthy, resilient and purposeful teams. This has been highlighted particularly within the health, social care and education workforce, where the overall aim is to look after or care for people's wellbeing. Working within these sectors has become progressively more difficult, with ever-increasing demands on services, and a pressure to do more for less. There are perpetual challenges with ongoing budget cuts and under-resourced services, which are having a detrimental impact on the services that leaders are trying to provide.

When working within services that primarily support people, there is also a wider challenge – the impact of systemic underlying societal factors, such as more people living in poverty, the financial crisis, societal behavioural changes due to the impact of technology, changes in expectations in society of public services, a decline in mental health, higher demands on, and therefore more limited access to, services, and therefore potentially higher thresholds to gain access to services. These factors, although perhaps not always directly linked to a leader's service, may further exacerbate the overall pressures that they are under. As we describe within Chapters 4 and 9, these pressures are felt not only by individuals, but also by teams and the organization as a whole, and can lead to a breakdown of safety and unhealthy behaviours. These stressors may then lead to an overwhelmed workforce, with poor staff wellbeing and burnout, and difficulties with recruitment and retention.

Given the context, it takes a leader who has a great deal of self-awareness, who takes time to truly understand their team and organizational behaviours, to consider what is needed and how best to proceed – a leader who has a systemic understanding, enables those around them to stretch themselves, and provides both care and challenge to the team. When this is done well, we would call this a *psychologically responsive leader*. When you can draw on psychologically responsive leadership skills, this enables you, as a leader, to build healthier, more purposeful and productive teams and organizations.

We have written his book for leaders (and aspiring leaders) within health, social care, education and related fields to develop their skills in psychologically responsive leadership. It was important to us that this book is accessible (translating our knowledge about psychological theory and approaches within leadership) and practical. We often read leadership books that can be really interesting and academic, and find ourselves nodding away, highlighting sections and writing notes, but then it can be tricky to know how to put what we have read into practice. In our experience, this is often frustrating when there is a disconnect between having knowledge and understanding and knowing how to put this into action in order to help ourselves, our teams and our organizations thrive. Therefore, we have written a book where we discuss key aspects of psychologically responsive leadership based on our extensive work with leaders within health, social care and education fields. We have presented the relevant theory in an accessible way, along with tips and approaches for leaders to apply this in their daily work. We have also captured examples of where these leadership principles have been applied well, within health, social care and education, but also within other areas – as good psychologically responsive leadership skills are highly transferable and relevant in all contexts. As you will see throughout the book, we have included tasks that you, as leaders, can utilize with your team to enable you to put your knowledge and skills into practice, and create spaces for your self-reflection, including an ongoing personal leadership development plan at the end of the book (see Chapter 10).

Therefore, if you are interested in the psychology of human behaviour (individuals, groups and systems) and how it can be applied to leadership, and if you want to develop a deeper understanding of yourself as a leader, in order to work towards becoming the best leader you can be, for yourself and for your team, then this is the book for you.

Defining psychologically responsive leadership

We define psychologically responsive leadership as 'drawing on current psychological theory and knowledge of humans as individuals and in groups, with a systemic perspective, to enhance the development and leadership of ourselves and others'. This helps us improve our wellbeing and performance as leaders, and that of our colleagues, which inevitably serves our clients too.

Psychologically responsive leaders have a fundamental interest in deepening their knowledge of human psychology and what helps to improve (or undermine) the performance and wellbeing of themselves and their team. They have an appetite for self-reflection and curiosity about other people's perspectives, valuing diversity of thought and an understanding of how and when to adapt their leadership style to the context. This includes being attuned to the needs of their team so that they can respond in a helpful way, while also holding in mind the wider context and organizational pressures. Being psychologically responsive also means recognizing that the dynamics of emotions and behaviour ripple between people and different levels of a system. They understand that what happens high up in an organization will impact those at other levels of the organization, and vice versa.

In the ever-changing world that we live and work within, with constantly shifting demands, pressures and opportunities, it is essential for leaders to take a systemic approach to their thinking. This means understanding the complex dynamics that occur both within a team and an organization, as well as dynamics from outside the organization (professional, cultural or political) that impact its functioning. Although we might have specific goals that we are working towards, for our teams and services, every aspect of our work will be impacted by what is happening throughout the wider system: from relational dynamics playing out within our teams or organizations (see Chapter 4) to political or societal changes (see Chapter 3). As we discover within Chapter 3, it is essential, as leaders, to have a good systemic understanding to be able to continue to assess the 'bigger picture' and future plan for success.

Where leaders can draw on psychological knowledge to consider the interplays between systemic factors, this can help them to be empathic and understanding, forward-thinking, agile and responsive to their context. Within this book, we will provide you with different methods to help you develop your skills for thinking systemically and understanding systemic dynamics as a leader. In Chapter 4 we will support you as a leader to develop an awareness of psychological and therapeutic models of wellbeing and relational dynamics. A good knowledge of these models can help us to better understand what we and our team are experiencing. This enables us to lead and navigate our team through challenging experiences and events in a proactive and informed manner. When we apply psychological thinking to our own development, we enhance our self-knowledge and awareness of our leadership. We are able to consider how we might be perceived by others, and how we might be a positive, or unintentionally unhelpful, influence on our team. This enhanced self-awareness can help us to consider how we might utilize our strengths, be mindful of any emotional pulls or challenges we encounter, work closely with others who have complementary skills, and continue to develop our own knowledge and expertise throughout our leadership journey. Self-reflection is key, and we have provided many opportunities and prompts for reflection throughout the book.

Within this book, we aim to give you the means to develop your understanding and practice of these skills, drawing from organizational, social and clinical psychology theory and practice. A psychologically responsive leader knows that we never stop developing, continuing to reflect and learning more about ourselves and those we work with. The process is never complete, so we should always be active and striving.

We use the term 'psychologically responsive' rather than 'trauma-informed' as we are concerned that the term 'trauma' has become overused, which has the potential to diminish real traumatic experience. In fact, we are often talking about a range of experiences, some of which may be traumatic and some of which are stressful or uncomfortable. When taking a 'psychologically responsive' perspective, we are thinking about our psychobiological threat system (often known as our 'fight, flight, freeze or flop' response), which shapes our sense of safety, trust, openness and confidence. But we are also thinking about other aspects of human behaviour too, such as interpersonal and systemic dynamics and how human behaviour is shaped through our positive or aversive experiences. Holding all of this information in mind when thinking about leadership helps us to be truly psychologically responsive.

What we cover within the book

Within this book, we will talk you through the essential elements of psychologically responsive leadership. The chapters follow the EVOLVING psychologically responsive leadership framework (described in more detail below), to explore how we can better Enable others, develop and embed Values and vision, Observe and understand the relational dynamics that we may see in our teams or systems, be aware of the power of Language and communicate well, be Vulnerable in a way that supports our teams while developing greater self-reflection, show genuine Integrity to build trust, use Narratives and storytelling positively in our leadership, and underlying it all, Generate feelings of safety and belonging within the teams we lead.

A crucial aspect of being a psychologically responsive leader is knowing how to motivate, enable and empower those we lead. In Chapter 1, we explore how we can use psychological theory to better understand the motivations and drives of individuals within our teams, to allow us to build on these factors, which can promote energy, enthusiasm, commitment and loyalty in our teams. We have also included a section on coaching, to support you to have helpful, enabling coaching conversations with your team. We then consider how best to 'lean into' discussions about performance, bring healthy challenge and integrate these practices into your team culture. We recognize that this is not always an easy thing to do, and so we discuss some of the psychological defences that can get in the way of giving or receiving difficult feedback, and think about ways to overcome these defences. We reflect on a leader's role in creating a sense of safety, belonging and connection within their team, and how important this is to enable the team to be creative, embrace opportunities to learn and develop, and take on new challenges. Lots of examples are given, with practical tips, to support you to embed these leadership practices within your team.

Chapter 2 explores how you, as a leader, can shape the mindset of your team to enable growth and innovation. We discuss that by supporting our teams to understand the psychology behind failure, and the differences between a fixed and growth mindset, we can start to view appropriate failure as an inherent part of endeavour and creativity. This perspective can enable us to be creative and 'think outside the box'. We also consider the power of systemic psychological thinking within groups, and how you might use this skill, as a leader, to promote shared understanding and collaborative working, to create successful and meaningful outcomes.

In Chapter 3, we focus on methods for leaders to build greater connection and cohesion within their teams and organizations through the development of an organizational vision, mission and shared values. We include lots of practical exercises for you, as a leader, which you can also use with your team. We draw on acceptance and commitment therapy (ACT) principles to think about the importance of purpose and values, for individuals, teams and organizations. We consider as leaders how we can support ourselves and our teams to create strategies to help us move purposely towards our shared team values in our work and recognize what might (unintentionally) pull us away or act as a barrier to us achieving this. We reflect on how a sense of connection and belonging within a team/organization, a shared purpose and shared values can positively impact individual wellbeing and feelings of self-worth, and promote agency and direction. Where staff can identify personal meaning within their work (such as having shared values or a shared purpose), this can help them to feel more confident in their work, and more loyal and committed to the overall vision and organizational goals. Within the chapter, we help you, as a leader, to reflect on the wider context, including considering likely future scenarios your team may encounter, and how to account for this within strategic planning. We know that when we have a clear and forward-thinking strategy that takes this into account, then, as leaders, we are more able to be agile, adaptable and resilient when we encounter new challenges, and are therefore more likely to be successful. This agility, adaptability and resilience also helps our team to feel more able to trust in us, as a leader.

One of the key elements of psychologically responsive leadership is developing skills for understanding ourselves and others. Within Chapter 4, we focus on the psychology of human behaviour within dyads, groups, teams and organizations to help you to understand some of the key behaviours and interactions that you may see play out within your team/organization. We also consider how you can work with and address these behaviours where appropriate. Being able to recognize and name the interpersonal dynamics at play between people, in couples, groups, teams or organizations, can help you, as a leader, to promote more positive dynamics and mitigate unhelpful ones. We also help you to reflect on your own likely 'pushes and pulls' within relationships, as we know that when leaders can reflect on these dynamics, it allows us to enhance our relationships with team members and colleagues. We explore psychological theory around the impact of trauma and stress on individuals, but also on teams and organizations. This knowledge can help us to recognize and name when 'parallel processes' could play out (where different levels of the organization 'mirror' each other in relation to thoughts, feelings and behaviours), and how we can step in and buffer against these effects. This then allows leaders to have more agency within these dynamics, and to be proactive in naming and addressing them. We end the chapter by thinking about the concept of 'resilience', both for individuals and within groups, teams and organizations. We explore the key factors central to resilience, and consider how this knowledge can help us to recover and even thrive, despite us experiencing stress and challenge. We hope that this chapter will give you many examples and topics to discuss within your teams, to enable you, as a leader, to help your team reflect on how they work together, any key relational challenges that might occur, how these might be addressed, and how to build your overall organizational resilience. In turn, this can help you to build a relationally healthy team.

Within Chapter 5, we develop a greater understanding of language, and communication in general, within leadership, including the power of cultural and dominant narratives and how these are often used (both intentionally and unintentionally) to include or exclude others. We recognize that good communication is a crucial skill of psychologically responsive leadership, and reflect on the influence that you have, as a leader, through your day-to-day communication with your team. Consideration of the individual communication needs of those you are leading (or leading with) can allow you to communicate more purposely and effectively, supporting your connection with your colleagues and your ability to support their development. We explain that it is essential in leadership to develop an awareness of your own emotional state moment to moment, so that you can be more in control of how you communicate, both verbally and non-verbally. Therefore, we also consider methods of self-regulation that can be helpful to utilize, both before and during important communications with others. These skills and knowledge can then help you feel more confident and emotionally contained in your communications, and more responsive in your leadership. Furthermore, we explore how being able to 'tune into' your team's emotional tone and recognizing what they might need at that moment (e.g., more energy, or feelings of safety/containment) enables you to support your team and move them to a more optimal emotional state. We break down what it means to be an 'engaging leader' and how you might demonstrate these skills within your communication. We reflect on what teams might need from leaders at a time of crisis, and how this may require a different communication style. Common challenges experienced by organizations, including those within the health, social care and education sectors, which can lead to a breakdown in communication/ineffective communication, are considered, along with how leaders might address these. We hope that this focus on communication will allow you to understand how you might improve your communication to get the best out of your team at different times and within different contexts.

Although we might wish, as leaders, to be seen as always knowing the answer and having endless confidence in our approach, this is neither realistic nor helpful, either for us as leaders or for our teams. In Chapter 6, we reflect on the importance of leaders showing some vulnerability and fallibility to their teams, while finding a balance on the 'vulnerability continuum', considering what is helpful to the people we are communicating with at the time. Where we can accept our vulnerability and see it as the underlying basis for 'courage', this allows us to take measured risks and acknowledge the challenges we face and how these may affect us as leaders. Consequently, we can then seek appropriate support and advice from others. These behaviours model to our team our perception of sharing some vulnerability as positive, and something that is likely to enhance, rather than hinder, our performance. Where we can take time to reflect on our own leadership, understand our unconscious drives and patterns of behaviour, acknowledge our strengths and areas for development, this can support us to be the best possible leaders we can be.

In Chapter 7, we explore what trust and integrity mean within leadership. To be vulnerable and self-reflective, we need to trust enough in ourselves and others that it is 'sufficiently safe' to be open and authentic. We explore some models of trust, and apply this to leadership. We aim to support you to enhance your feelings of trust in yourself as a leader and build trusting relationships within your team. We need to feel trust and safety within our relationships in order to continue to learn and develop and perform at our best. Integrity is often cited as a highly regarded quality in leadership, and it is an integral part of being a psychologically responsive leader. We need to show our integrity in order to build trust in our relationships. Within the chapter we provide lots of opportunities for you to reflect on your own leadership, what helps you to build and maintain trust, and the impact this can have on relationships within your team. We then ask you to consider which areas of trust might be strengths for you, and other areas you might want to develop and focus on further.

Within Chapter 8, we start to pull together all your learning and self-reflections from the previous chapters, to build a narrative around your own personal leadership story and the story of your team or organization. We consider how influential and compelling storytelling is to humans, and how it is a prominent part of our history and our future as we use it to create meaning of our human experience. As leaders, if you can harness the power of storytelling and use it within your day-to-day practice, it can be an incredibly useful skill. We explore how you can use storytelling to co-create a shared purpose with your team, to show appropriate vulnerability and self-awareness, and communicate in an effective and engaging manner. We also describe several ways to co-create stories with your team that can strengthen connections, understandings of ourselves and our journeys and of each other, a sense of belonging to the organization or team, and a sense of being 'in it together'. We recognize within this chapter that stories can also have additional benefits in supporting ourselves as leaders, and our teams, to talk about and process challenges that we face, or have faced, and can enable us to 'heal' after difficult, or even traumatic, experiences. We give some practical examples and considerations of how you can take this forward in your leadership journey.

For teams to feel able to engage in authentic, exploratory story-telling and share their own experiences, they need to feel safe enough to do so. Chapter 9 builds on earlier chapters focusing on integrity and trust (Chapter 7), vulnerability (Chapter 6) and team dynamics (Chapter 4) to help you to contemplate where your team may currently sit with regard to feelings of psychological safety, and the actions you can take to develop great psychological safety. This chapter on psychological safety is situated towards the end of the book as it draws together many of the aspects of psychologically responsive leadership discussed throughout the book, and articulates how they apply to psychological safety.

We outline the history of the term 'psychological safety' and how it became more prominent following a number of studies investigating the key factors that differentiated the most effective teams. We think about what psychological safety is and what it is not and what is meant by 'interpersonal risk', and help you to consider how factors at an individual, team, professional, organizational and societal level may impact how safe individuals in your team may feel to 'speak up'. This will allow you to build a psychological, systemic understanding of safety within your team or organization, and what might help or hinder this. We recognize that safety is dynamic and ever-changing, and that we therefore need to continuously reflect on and build this up. We then explore how you, as a leader, can help to 'generate' a sense of safety within your team and organization, to create a more psychologically responsive environment.

The final chapter of the book (Chapter 10) then gives you the opportunity to summarize your reflections and learning from each chapter, to create a personal psychologically responsive leadership development plan. We have created this outline plan to help you to utilize your personal and key reflections from the book, consider your individual intentions and put them into practice. The plan is divided into sections that map on to the book chapters, to structure your thinking regarding key aspects of leadership – both in terms of yourself as a leader and in the context of your team and organization. As a psychologically responsive leader it is helpful to create the time and space to think, reflect and take on new information and then consider how to use this information in the future, make a plan and decide how you will hold yourself accountable. This is important in order to keep your leadership EVOLVING.

Throughout the book, we have included many practical activities with which to engage your team or organization in order to support their development, growth, cohesion and wellbeing. There are also self-reflection activities and prompts. There are several case examples, and some of these have been anonymized to protect confidentiality. You may also find it useful to listen to some of the EVOLVING psychologically responsive leadership podcast episodes[1] alongside the chapters (available on most podcast platforms). We hope you will find the information, ideas and examples useful in your leadership development.

A NOTE ON THE EVOLVING PSYCHOLOGICALLY RESPONSIVE LEADERSHIP FRAMEWORK

We decided to devise a framework to outline the key elements of psychologically responsive leadership, drawn from our knowledge and experience of organizational psychology and clinical psychology, and we named this framework

---

1   See, for example, https://podcasters.spotify.com/pod/show/evolvingleads

'EVOLVING'. We chose this name as we felt that its definition accurately reflected the ongoing development process
of becoming a good psychologically responsive leader: 'To
develop/evolve a style of one's own... To change or develop...
into an improved or more advanced state.' Being a leader is
all about learning (including becoming more self-aware),
adapting and continuing to evolve.

Enabling others

Vision and values

Observing relational dynamics

Language and communication

Vulnerability and self-reflection

Integrity and trust

Narratives: personal and organizational

Generating psychological safety

The EVOLVING psychologically responsive leadership framework

The EVOLVING psychologically responsive leadership framework provides the basis for our eight-day leadership course
that we run in person, and our psychological consultation,
training and coaching to individuals, teams and organizations.[2] The framework is also the basis for this book as we
pull together what we have learned from our work, reading,
and discussion with leaders and our guests on our EVOLVING
podcast. The chapters therefore follow the structure of the
course, with the aim of building up the reader's psychological knowledge and understanding as they work through the
chapters.

---

2   See https://cmcafs.com/evolving-leadership

CHAPTER 1

Enabling Others: Connecting and Coaching

Being a leader is a tough job. Sometimes we can make it even tougher on ourselves by believing that we should know everything and always have the right answers and the skills we need for success. This is not realistic. What we have learned is that the best psychologically responsive leaders work *with* others, recognize, encourage and develop strengths within others, and consult with their teams to get a shared understanding of how to progress. They recognize that they cannot do it alone. It is important to have contingency and succession plans, so that we know that we can 'step back' and encourage our team to take a lead where needed. In addition, the more that we can develop good, psychologically responsive leadership skills within our teams, the more motivated, connected and effective our teams as a whole are likely to be.

When we are thinking about 'enabling others', there is a shift from focusing solely on our own leadership skills to thinking about how we develop and support others to build their confidence, skills and capacity to reach their potential. Perhaps before reading this chapter take a few minutes to reflect on who has helped, inspired or encouraged you to develop your leadership journey (formally or informally). Consider:

- How did they do this?

- What did you find most helpful?

- What did you value about their approach?
- What was the impact of their approach on you?

The context

At the time of writing, with the aftermath of the pandemic and financial stress on individuals, families and services, we know that the health, social care and education workforce is generally feeling depleted, overstretched and lacking energy, and sometimes burnt out. In addition, people's view of the world and personal values have started to shift to prioritize their health and wellbeing and that of their families. For example, the 2022 Microsoft Work Trend Index Annual Report found that when asked about their views of work pre- and post-pandemic, 53 per cent of employees said that they would now be more likely to prioritize health and wellbeing over work (including 55 per cent of parents and 56 per cent of women). In addition, 52 per cent of younger generations within the workplace (known as 'Gen Z' and 'Millennials') said that they were likely to consider changing their employer that year. Microsoft concluded that employees are now considering their 'worth it equation', balancing the demands of work with what they get from being employed within that particular role. What people value within the workplace has also shifted, with many more people requesting flexibility in hours and hybrid or remote working.

It is therefore even more important to consider how we help our teams to feel energized and engaged, that their work is meaningful, that their skills are being utilized, and that it is 'worth it' to be part of our team. How we help colleagues to feel valued and connected with one another is also a question many leaders are grappling with, and is also relevant to how we develop and enable our teams.

Talking about it

One of the most impactful things that you can do to build positive relationships with your employees and colleagues is to show a genuine interest in them, their role and their development. The word 'genuine' is important as it is integral to the building of trust (see Chapter 7). People are intuitive and recognize when the interest of others is performative. And if they don't realize immediately, they soon will. Instead, being curious about the person with whom you are working and asking impactful questions can help them to know that they matter, both to you and the organization. For people you directly manage and supervise, regular conversations with them (both informal catch-ups and more structured meetings, such as appraisals and personal development planning) can be ways to find out more about them, their strengths, their views on work, the challenges they are facing (both inside and outside work), their values and what is important to them, their hopes and wants for the future, what motivates them, and how you can maximize their potential. Therefore, being interested and curious about others is a significant factor in leadership.

It is important for us, as leaders, to offer space for these conversations, as although people often want to talk about their roles and their hopes for development and progression, they may not feel comfortable requesting the conversation. Having routine conversations can be very useful to create space for regular feedback, planning, coaching and keeping on track. They can also be really motivating for the individual, who will appreciate that you are invested in their development and future in your team. They can offer an opportunity to 'notice and name' if you have observed someone's motivation at work appearing to drift. Where this is apparent, you can check in promptly to support and address this – which means you can start to gain a greater understanding of what might be happening and what the team member might need in order to be fully engaged at work again.

Informal check-ins, formal supervision and regular meetings provide the foundations for understanding our team members and their work, skills and potential.

Psychological enrichment

What can inspire, challenge and motivate us at work? What is the 'fuel' that drives and excites us, and keeps us turning up? Although some of this can be individual and linked to personal values (see Chapter 3), there are several key areas that we can consider in supporting our team to thrive. It can also be useful to reflect on how this applies to you. What drives, inspires and motivates you at work? This can then help you to make sure that you have a good balance that will keep you engaged and motivated in work, and that you can dip into even more if you start to feel uninspired (which happens to us all at times).

An integral psychological theory around motivation is self-determination theory (SDT) (Deci, Olafsen and Ryan 2017), which postulates that when we satisfy our needs for competence, autonomy and relatedness, this can create a state of optimal motivation, which helps us to function, learn and perform at our best, and can positively impact our wellbeing. SDT assumes that people naturally want to learn and grow, and will seek out opportunities to do this. However, sometimes the world that we live in, or the organizations or context that we work in, can get in the way of, or create obstacles preventing, our basic psychological needs for autonomy, competence and relatedness. As stated by Legault (2017, p.4694), 'As a consequence of this person-environment interplay, people become either engaged, curious, connected, and whole, or demotivated, ineffective, and detached.'

What do we mean by autonomy, competence and relatedness?

- *Autonomy:* I have choice and a sense of agency around what is done and how it is done; I can work independently, make my own decisions and determine my own actions.

- *Competence:* I feel effective and confident; I know what I need to do and how to do it; I have the skills needed to do my role well, to succeed and to work towards my goals.

- *Relatedness:* I feel closely connected with others around me; I feel that I matter and belong, and I feel comfortable to ask for help or support if needed.

Meeting these psychological needs at work

There are many ways we can meet these needs dependent on role and context, but here are some common examples of potential ways to increase drive and motivation in your team:

Autonomy

- A project you can get stuck into (either something that you can lead or have a key role in, or something you can collaborate with others around).

- An opportunity to take a lead on something you usually would not.

- Involvement in decision making or leading on decisions in a particular area.

- Taking on a new responsibility that is in line with your future hopes for work.

Competence

- When working on long-term projects, or where work does not have regular positive outcomes or feedback (where it can feel like you are getting nowhere fast), having the opportunity to do something where there are also some 'quick wins'.

- Being involved in something where your skills are going to be really utilized/valued can enhance feelings of competence.

- Getting positive feedback on something that is important to you or that has used your individual strengths and skills can also engender competence.

- Constructive feedback that can support you to develop your skills in a particular area, with the opportunities to put this into practice.

- Learning something completely new can be highly motivating.

- Having the opportunity to develop your skills in a particular area of interest.

- When you have led on a project, having the opportunity to take ownership of your work, and present the outcome to people higher up in the organization (rather than a manager presenting the work).

- New challenges with a bit of 'stretch' (but not too much – a challenge that is developmentally appropriate and achievable).

- Support to learn new skills without fear of failure – where you are shown what to do, have the opportunity to undertake the task collaboratively, do the task yourself while being prompted, and are then able to take it on independently (we call this 'show, do, prompt, step back').

Relatedness

- An opportunity to collaborate with a colleague or a team.

- Good team relationships, which feel supportive and collaborative, can lead to feelings of relatedness.

- Feeling (shared) ownership around a project or plan.

- Being part of things that matter (to you personally).

- The opportunity to create, innovate or co-create (see Chapter 2).

SDT also recognizes the power of 'intrinsic' motivation on behaviour, and acknowledges that where a person can receive intrinsic rewards (e.g., where they feel enjoyment or satisfaction, or a sense of achievement, because the behaviour was personally meaningful for them), this can lead to greater feelings of positivity and motivation. Therefore, our own enjoyment, sense of achievement and personal meaning can be big motivational factors. Alternatively, environments where individuals feel criticized or micromanaged, where there are cliques, or unhealthy competition between colleagues, can be highly demotivating, as this can lead to autonomy, a sense of competence and relatedness being diminished.

Giving feedback

When giving feedback, there is a clear difference between the aims and likely outcomes of more positive or more negative feedback. We may be drawn to giving negative feedback instinctively, since in our leadership role we are constantly thinking about how to improve performance and address any problems. We might be quite prudent in our thinking, where we are trying to avoid things going wrong. The ability to give positive developmental feedback well can be a real skill and one we can develop.

When giving more negative feedback we are typically trying to improve performance through naming and working through weaknesses or apparent 'deficits' for that individual, so all we can hope for is to get them to an average level of competence. Although this can be useful and important (when given with care), and can improve performance to some extent, by itself, it is not going to help us to get the best out of the individual. As humans, we tend to have a negativity bias, and there is a danger that we tune into the negative feedback that we receive, and ignore or even forget the positive feedback. This can then give us a negatively skewed point of view about how we are perceived. Over time, when all the feedback that we are receiving feels negative or critical, this can lead to feelings of resentment, a lack of motivation and a decline in performance. However, positive, strengths-based feedback focuses on something that we already know is a strength of that individual, and therefore the potential is much bigger. When we target and help the individual to harness and build on these strengths, we could potentially be helping them to excel in an area.

As leaders, it can therefore be helpful to lean into positive feedback even more, ensuring that your employees are aware that you recognize their real strengths and are working with them to see how they can be nurtured and utilized within their role and beyond, and how they can be an asset to the team. We cannot assume that our employees know that we value them and the strengths that they bring, so it is important to let them know, while doing this in a genuine and realistic way.

Giving positive feedback well

There are many ways in which we can give positive feedback, but there are a few things that it can be useful to consider:

- *How does the individual like to receive feedback?* Some people feel energized and appreciated when positive comments are made about them within a group setting, acknowledging their contribution. However, others may want to hide in a corner, disappear or run away. Some people prefer a private conversation, or a short message or email. However, unless an individual is extremely aversive to public acknowledgements of their good work, some discomfort in receiving public praise should not necessarily be a barrier to doing this. Sometimes people feel uncomfortable with public praise due to a lack of self-esteem, and part of building that self-esteem can be providing positive feedback on both an individual and public basis.

- *What does the individual see as important?* Feedback is likely to feel more meaningful and have a greater positive impact if it is on something that the individual really values. When you know which skills and values are important to them, personally, it gives you a better understanding of what they will view as meaningful. For example, you might compliment someone on their efficiency, but actually they do not see this as important – they would have felt more appreciated if you had complimented them on how they had shared a new, half-formed idea in a recent meeting (as this is something that they have been pushing themselves to do more).

- *How can we ensure that the feedback feels genuine?* There is a danger that if we accept that positive comments are important, we can overuse them without really thinking about why we are complimenting the person. Be more specific, such as pointing to a behaviour that you have witnessed, or a piece of feedback that you have heard about the individual, or a change that you have noticed. This can make the feedback feel more genuine and meaningful for the individual. Where possible, use real examples that explain the behaviour that you want to highlight, but also say why it is appreciated.

- *What about when we cannot think of anything to highlight that is positive?* It might be that you have had lots of negative feedback about the individual, so it can be hard to pick out any positives. Or perhaps they seem to be doing the bare minimum and not much more. Or perhaps you don't really know enough about them and their role. In these cases, it can be useful to spend time with that individual and be curious about their experience of their role and what they are working towards. Questions such as 'What have you been working towards recently?' or 'What have you been working on that you feel quite proud of?' or 'How have you managed to overcome some of the challenges that you have been facing?' can help you to start to pick out skills that they may have used, what they want to work towards, or things that are important to them.

- *Recognize effort, rather than solely results.* Where you can recognize the efforts that someone has demonstrated (whether the outcome has been successful or not) can be highly motivating and build confidence. For example, if someone had been working hard on a bid, and had put in a lot of work and thought, acknowledging their hard work (despite the outcome) can be validating and encouraging. It can make them more likely to put in effort regardless of the outcome in the future. It also helps them to build their confidence associated with their endeavour rather than simply the results of their efforts, which builds resilience. Resilience leads to a willingness to try new things, be creative and 'have a go' when there are no guarantees, which can have a significant and positive impact on overall performance.

Wigan Warriors Rugby League club: Praising endeavour rather than outcome

Matt Peet has been head coach of Wigan Warriors Rugby League team for just over two seasons (at the time of writing, 2024), and within this time, he has led them to win all four of the highest possible honours in Rugby League (Grand Final, Challenge Cup, Super League Leader's Shield and, most recently, the World Club Challenge).

There are many aspects of Matt's leadership that have been recognized, such as his being named Super League Coach of the Year in 2022 and receiving a further nomination in 2023. Matt prioritizes learning, higher purpose (community impact) and group connection above all else in his leadership. In addition to these areas, one of the things that really stands out has been how he recognizes and praises the endeavour and effort of the team as opposed to solely the outcome.

When Matt is asked post-match his views of his team's performance, he may seem slightly dismissive about the outcome or score of the game overall, instead recognizing the effort of the players, taking pride in how they 'turned up' and applied themselves. When preparing for games, Matt focuses less on the factors potentially out of their control, such as the likely performance of the opposition, but more on ensuring that the players put the work in during the week, so that they can play to the best of their ability and do themselves proud. The team's work ethic and dedication during training is acknowledged and celebrated. Then, during the match, Matt encourages the players not to feel pressure, but to try to enjoy it and take pride in their performance instead.

- *Recognize the power of colleagues' feedback.* As well as positive feedback from the leader, one of the most powerful forms of feedback is when it comes from colleagues. Knowing that their colleagues view them in a positive way, and recognize the effort and skill that they bring, can help people to feel a greater sense of connection and achievement, and know that they are valued within the wider team. Therefore, it can be helpful to find ways in which a colleague recognition process can be embedded.

iMap (individuals Making autism positive): Colleague recognition

Beth Davies, CEO of iMap, recently put a process in place to embed colleague recognition across the organization. On a quarterly basis, iMap asks its staff to consider nominating colleagues for its awards, under the categories of 'Understand', 'Empower' and 'Aspire' (which are linked to the company's ethos – 'Through understanding, we will empower each individual to achieve their aspirations'). iMap acknowledges, 'It's so important to recognize staff for their achievements, small or large, as we know many of them "go that extra mile" for both our service users and their colleagues', and suggests that these nominations are a great opportunity to show appreciation and recognition.

Considerations when giving developmental feedback

Within leadership, there are times when it is crucial to give timely, honest, developmental feedback. Although we may sometimes understandably want to avoid these conversations, we know that when we do, this can lead to problems building up over time and becoming even more problematic. Avoiding saying what we need to say can also lead to feelings of surprise, resentment and frustration between individuals and even throughout the team. There is then a danger that when we finally address the problem, the dam opens and the volume and intensity of our communication is unhelpful, which we later regret. This can then put us on the back foot, trying to explain or apologize for how things have come across or why we did not address the issue earlier. Furthermore, by not having timely upfront conversations about performance challenges, we are not giving the individual the chance to make changes or improve their performance. We should be clear and direct about these difficulties, while also expressing confidence in the person's ability to change their behaviour. Our support for them will give them the best possible chance to evolve and realize their potential.

We find that sometimes leaders are hesitant to do this, perhaps due to a fear of upsetting the team member, a hope that the problem will 'go away on its own' or worries about how the other person will react (perhaps reacting in a defensive or aggressive way). Many who work in the health, education and social care professions are caring, nurturing and encouraging individuals who may find having to critique or challenge their colleagues difficult. However, when these 'difficult conversations' are avoided, or pushed back, this can lead to problems snowballing and unhelpful patterns of behaviour and performance becoming the norm, and can have a negative impact on relationships within the team. As the leader you might feel some resentment towards the person, with the possibility that their behaviour or performance will not improve, and you might see an adverse knock-on effect within the team. Others may also see that you are 'allowing' this behaviour or poor performance to continue without challenge. This may impact their view of you, as the leader. Furthermore, by not talking this through with the individual in a timely way, you will be failing them, as you are denying them the opportunity to develop. Tell them what is not working, and what needs to improve, and how they can do this with your support. Without this approach it is unlikely that they are going to improve their performance and they may continue to feel a sense that they are getting things wrong, or not performing at their best. When we 'lean into' these conversations, it allows for an open honest discussion, which gives the person the best chance to improve their performance and feel supported in doing so.

There are, however, some things you might want to consider when giving developmental feedback. If developmental feedback is not done with care, it can lead to colleagues feeling under threat. Everyone will deal with developmental feedback in different ways, and some will be more able to listen to and accept it, whereas others may be more easily triggered into a threat or shame response.

The psychology of threat and shame

There are several ways in which getting negative feedback could lead to us feeling under threat. This can include feeling criticized or judged, 'bad', wrong or not good enough, when we feel that our relationship with the other person (or others in the wider team) might be compromised, or that our job might be affected. From a brain-based perspective, when we perceive a potential threat, our body quickly starts to react to this. Adrenaline is pumped around the body to prepare us to fight, flight, freeze or flop (or other threat-based responses). This means that our heart starts to race, our breathing quickens or temporarily stops (we gasp and hold our breath), our muscles become tense, and we become hypervigilant to any changes or potential threats in our environment. We are likely to be on edge, jumpy, and on the lookout for things going wrong. We may feel ready to defend ourselves or attack (including verbally), or we may feel the urge to get away from what is happening. All this is a primitive response that attempts to give us the best chance of survival, which, in the days of sabre-toothed tigers, it probably would have!

At the same time, our brains are also focused on survival. This means that the prefrontal cortex of the brain (the part that is involved in thinking, planning, reflecting, being able to see the bigger picture, regulating our emotions, connecting with others and considered decision making) goes 'offline', and instead our behaviour is governed by the more primitive part of the brain. Therefore, when we feel under threat, we are less likely to be able to think clearly, have thoughtful conversations with others, stay engaged or make good decisions. We may also hear what is said in a negatively biased way, as we are primed to pick up potential threats. When we are feeling under threat, we may also struggle to make sense of what is being said, and may leave a conversation feeling confused, perhaps having a different view of the conversation, or missing some information.

Another way that people may react to more negative feedback is a shame or defensive response. Shame is one of the most uncomfortable emotions that we have, and, as humans, we try everything that we can to defend against it. When we feel shame, we have a tendency to deny ('That's not true, I haven't done that'), blame someone else

('I was only late with the report because Dan didn't send the data on time'), minimize ('Okay, but I've only missed that one deadline') or feel 'rage'. Feeling rage can then lead us to feeling extreme anger or frustration, and may lead to us verbally or physically acting in an aggressive or intimidating manner.

The other problem with shame is that it makes us feel *personally* attacked, that is, that we are bad, as opposed to our behaviour or performance being bad or critiqued. The problem here is that being 'bad' is perceived as an unchangeable characteristic that the person has (in all situations and across time), whereas if the behaviour is bad, rather than the person, it is likely to be perceived as context-specific (and less linked to the inherent nature of the person and their worth) and therefore more open to change. So, if the feedback is triggering a shame or threat response, it is unlikely to be particularly helpful.

Making developmental feedback enabling and not threatening or shaming

There are many ideas that we will share in this area, but underlying them all is the power of the relationship. Having good, trusting relationships with in-built psychological safety (see Chapter 9) will put you in the best position to be able to talk about difficult topics with, and give feedback to, your team. It can be useful to embed regular upfront conversations with feedback, or encourage your team members to seek feedback from others, so that these become part of the everyday culture of the team, and where feedback is seen as an opportunity to learn and continue to develop.

In addition to seeking feedback from others, it can also be helpful to have space for individuals to reflect on their own work, to consider where they feel that their strengths might lie, and what they could improve on and how.

Individual debriefs

Embedding individual debriefs into day-to-day practice can also be a helpful tool and a great way of enabling reflection. Within elite sport, coaches often schedule individual 'catch-ups' after a sporting event. These are set up to be like a structured coaching session, where the individual has an opportunity to reflect on their own performance, in a non-judgemental space (see the section 'Coaching conversations' later in this chapter for more information and guidance about coaching). The athlete can reflect on what went well and how they utilized their strengths or put prior learning into practice. They can also reflect on what did not go as well and what might have got in the way of them performing at their best (which could be a range of factors, including internal ones such as self-doubt or being distracted, or external factors such as the weather on the day of the event or poor sleep the night before), and ways in which they could improve next time, setting themselves intentions or goals around this. Using this method puts the focus on self-development, it can enhance feelings of mastery, ownership and responsibility, and can be motivating and empowering.

High care, high challenge

We often talk about high care, high challenge. This is when we find the balance of providing challenge and constructive feedback along with support and care, which is associated with high performance. From a psychological perspective, when an individual feels understood and supported by another, it increases their sense of safety. This, in turn, makes it easier for them to remain emotionally regulated and engaged in conversation without getting caught up in a shame or threat response. When we feel safe, we are more able to access our prefrontal cortex (the 'thinking' part of our brain), allowing us to see the bigger picture, reflect, empathize, engage in discussion, consider things carefully and make better decisions. If we feel supported, we also feel more confident to try something new and push ourselves out of our comfort zone, which can enable us to take on challenges and promotes high performance.

THE IMPORTANCE OF HIGH CARE, HIGH CHALLENGE

- *Care without challenge:* 'I know that Sarah[1] is having a hard time at home right now and is struggling with the recent changes in her role. Her performance at work has slipped, but it's understandable, so I won't say anything as I don't want to make things feel even more difficult for her.'

- *Challenge without care:* 'Sarah's work is not up to standard, and I will be direct and let her know that it needs to improve, and give her a timescale for this, as she is currently underperforming.'

- *No challenge, no care:* 'I don't have time to address this as I have enough on. Sarah will just have to work it out herself and improve, or the rest of the team are going to get frustrated with her.'

- *Care with challenge:* 'I need to have a conversation with Sarah about her performance. First, I'll check in with her and find out her views of what is happening and what might be affecting her performance (so that I have a greater understanding of what the issue is), and what might help. Then, I'll give clear expectations of what needs to improve, and we can come up with a shared plan around this.'

TIPS FOR PREPARING FOR A DIFFICULT CONVERSATION

- Consider what you want to get out of the conversation – what is the desired outcome?

- Think about where the conversation is held – such as somewhere private and calm, where you are unlikely to be distracted. Wherever possible, a meeting in person (rather

---

1   A made-up name, for purposes of anonymity.

than online) is preferable as this improves connection and ability to read non-verbal communication.

- Consider when you have the discussion – think about who is likely to be present at that time, and the person's commitments during that day. If you have the meeting early in the day, it might be that the person will be preoccupied with what was discussed all day. This might be problematic. However, if you have the meeting at the end of the day, the person (and you) may be left with unresolved feelings if the discussion ends abruptly or in a difficult manner. Make sure that you have the chance to check in with the person again afterwards, if needed.

- Think about who is present for the conversation, and who needs to be there. If there are more than two of you, discuss prior to the meeting who is going to take the lead, and who is going to say what, to ensure that you are on the same page.

- If you know your member of staff well, you might feel more able to tailor it to make it feel easier for them. For example, it might be that going for a walk with one member of staff while talking would be helpful, whereas another might prefer to meet in a quiet place in the office. Similarly, some people's preferred ways of working might mean that they will want lots of detailed information to understand what you are trying to communicate to them (see Chapter 5 on language and communication). They may want time to process it, whereas others might want to focus more on what immediate actions they can take.

- Similarly, think about your commitments for that day, and what you will be doing afterwards. You will need to bring your 'best self' to this meeting. It can be helpful if you can make sure that you have what you need to remain regulated and calm throughout. You might also want to plan in a check-in/debrief with a colleague afterwards.

- As Caroline Twitchett (in our EVOLVING podcast episode on observing and understanding relational dynamics) talked about,[2] 'sometimes you just need to "put on your big girl pants" (or equivalent!) and get through it'. It might feel uncomfortable, but remind yourself that it is important, needed and the right thing to do, and it is a crucial skill to develop as a leader.

- Think through and plan out what the key messages are, and how you can get them across clearly (perhaps write these down to keep you on track). Be clear and upfront – frame the conversation and what it is about.

- Try to find a balance where you are providing candour but avoiding being 'brutally honest'. Try to make sure that you are focusing on the behaviour rather than the person themselves. Be as specific as possible. For example, rather than 'You make people feel uncomfortable in our team meetings,' try 'I have noticed that sometimes you have rolled your eyes after people have spoken in team meetings. This behaviour can make people feel uncomfortable or judged.'

- If possible, it can be useful to talk it through with a colleague, sharing what you are hoping to say, getting their feedback on how it comes across, and anything you might want to consider further.

- Remain open – although you might have some ideas of what you want to get across, it is important that you are open to the other person's views. Use it as a way of exploring the member of staff's perspective, remaining as curious as possible. You can accept that this is their view, even if you do not agree with it yourself. When you have gathered information through your discussions with them, and you

2   See https://podcasters.spotify.com/pod/show/evolvingleads/episodes/ Observing-Relational-Dynamics-e1p2etm

start to understand things from their point of view (even if it differs from your own), it can help you to think about possible ways forward. It can also help them to feel understood, which can bring you towards each other within the discussion, and make both you and them less defensive.

- Be clear with any expectations – explain the rationale, and what exactly you are wanting them to do, how and when. The more precise and clear you are, the better. People can often struggle to know what to do when they are told that their behaviour or work is not okay and needs to improve but are not given clear guidance of what the leader wants it to change to and how they can get there.

- Affirm them – in the discussion, it can help to remind the person why they are personally important to you, the team and the organization, and why you want them to succeed (acknowledging that you believe that they can, and this is why you are giving them feedback).

- Where appropriate, bring yourself into the conversation by showing a little empathy and vulnerability – for example, recognizing that you, too, have found some of these things tough at times.

- Problem solve together: 'How can we resolve this? What do you need from me to make this work?' When thinking about how to address the issue, after gaining a fuller understanding, try to think with them about how 'we' can take this forward. Shared ownership can be a useful way of thinking about what steps they need to take, and how you (or others) can support them with this to make it successful.

- Name the desired outcome: if these things are put in place, or these changes are made, this will be the outcome.

- Make sure that there is an agreed time frame for objectives, and that regular catch-ups are booked in to ensure that things stay on track and any obstacles can be addressed early. You will want to ensure that you have given them the best chance of success.

- Be ready to bring things back to the discussion, and the purpose of the conversation, as there is a danger that the conversation may go off on a tangent. This is why preparing and having a few key points written down in advance can be helpful.

- Prepare for how you will bring the meeting to an end as well as possible. If the person has a defensive response and, despite your best efforts, they are unable to acknowledge the situation, it can be helpful to focus on your understanding that this is difficult for them to hear and that you would like you both to reflect on how you can resolve the difficulties and move forward together.

- Physical movement can help us transition and move on from an uncomfortable experience. Planning the opportunity to engage in physical activity, to walk or move between spaces after a difficult conversation, can help both you and your colleague to process the difficult feelings a little.

- It can be useful to have an opportunity to check in a few days later. This can help to repair any relational challenges following the meeting, but also ensure the person's understanding and give them the opportunity to ask any follow-up questions.

When all else fails...

There will be times when you have put time and effort into supporting someone in their role, you have had clear upfront discussions with them about their performance and what needs to change (and have given them time and help to change things), and it is still not working. It might be that the person is just not a good fit for the role, the team or organization, or their behaviour is of concern, and these things can have a detrimental impact on team dynamics. You might then be at a stage where you need to consider performance management.

It can be tempting to hope that things will get better and to delay having these conversations. However, we know that when poor behaviour is tolerated or ignored, it is likely to continue or even get worse. Therefore, we would recommend that in these cases it can be useful to get some HR or legal support to make sure that you have thought everything through.

360-degree feedback

We are personally big fans of 360-degree feedback, and we use it a lot in our work. This is when questionnaires (usually anonymous) are sent to people who work closely with the individual at different levels (e.g., their manager, colleagues, those they supervise or manage, clients) to ask for feedback on their performance in a range of areas. As an important part of being a psychologically responsive leader is continually developing and enhancing your self-awareness, this can also be a great tool to gain a greater understanding of how you yourself are perceived by others. Questionnaires can include feedback on the individual's interactions with others, their strengths and what they bring to their role, the team and wider organization, what potential they might have that may be untapped, and what their areas for development could be. If you are struggling for questions, why not create them around your organization's key competencies, with space to identify the individual's particular strengths and potential areas for development?

As clinical psychologists, we have learned so much from the 360-degree feedback that we have received from peers, supervisors, supervisees, those we work with, wider connections and people who have had the opportunity to observe our work. It can challenge us, and our perceptions, creating a deeper understanding, which allows us to then think about how we develop. There are pros and cons to this feedback being anonymous, as it can be difficult when you receive feedback that you want to act on but cannot get further clarity on what has been said. On the other hand, anonymity is likely to allow respondents to be more open and honest in their feedback.

We find that, over time, if 360s are done regularly (once or twice a year), people get used to giving more honest feedback as they see how their responses are influential. It can be helpful to know who is saying what, so that you can talk to them about it, being curious and open to finding out more from them. It can also give you context as to their responses. However, when responses are anonymous, it can sometimes allow people to say things that they would not say otherwise. In general, anonymous feedback allows individuals to be more open and honest with their feedback, although it may be that individuals with a grudge also make use of this anonymity to be 'brutal' or unfair. When sending out the questionnaire, you can set the scene, letting people know that you want them to be honest and open in their feedback, and how you want to use it to support your self-awareness and further development.

If you adopt this procedure with your team, please consider doing it for yourself, too. Where you can 'model the model', this shows your team that you really believe in the process and are open to their feedback too.

> A note of caution: If you ask your team for feedback of any kind, please make sure that you acknowledge their responses, and, where appropriate, talk about how you are going to take things forward or not (and why).

Sarah was once part of a multidisciplinary team where they were asked to complete a heavy, long, online form about the team she was in. This concerned team dynamics, the leadership and culture, and what the team thought should be improved and how. They were told that there would be some feedback after a few weeks, and then a development plan would be put in place. The team invested a lot of time and effort into completing the form and were open, and potentially vulnerable, in their responses, talking about some of the challenges within the team, with the hope that this would be taken forward. A few weeks, then months, went by. Nothing happened. Several members of the team asked the leadership team when they would be getting feedback and when the actions would be put in place. They were told, 'Ah, we decided not to use that in the end.' The team felt frustrated, powerless and exposed. It also impacted on team engagement, as they were less trusting that future interventions would go ahead, and had a sense that the leadership team had perhaps not wanted to hear what had been said, so they had chosen to ignore it. Even if this was not the case, these perceptions had impacted negatively on team morale and relationships with the leadership team.

Creating feelings of belonging

Belonging can be defined as 'The subjective feeling of deep connection with social groups, physical places, and individual and collective experiences' (Allen *et al.* 2021, p.87). As clinical psychologists, we know that having a sense of belonging is a key factor for wellbeing and resilience. A key human need is to be 'known and understood', and this helps us to feel we belong. Being part of something shared, feeling accepted within a relationship or a group, and feeling connected to those around us impacts positively on our wellbeing and our sense of self, and our ability to get through difficult times. Furthermore, when we feel that we belong at work, this impacts on our feelings about the workplace and our role as well as our wellbeing and happiness more generally. We are more likely to be loyal and committed to our team and organization and may feel psychologically safer (see Chapter 9) to speak up and bring our views and perspectives. This also has a knock-on effect in terms of our likelihood of remaining in our job, and improves our performance at work overall (with a study by Carr *et al.* (2019) finding that feelings of belonging at work led to a 56 per cent increase in job performance, a 50 per cent decrease in risk of staff turnover and a 75 per cent drop in sickness leave).

We sometimes talk about the idea of 'belonging cues', which can show how connected individuals in a team or organization may feel to each other. As well as showing colleagues within the team that they are valued and that they belong, these cues can also signal to others outside of the organization, or new people joining the team, how the group functions, and may give them a sense of safety to join in too. These cues show safety between colleagues across a team where everyone can interact with anyone else, and there are no cliques or 'in' and 'out' groups that can lead to people feeling on the outside or excluded. Instead, everyone feels included and part of something. There are often lots of little, playful interactions, and opportunities to have fun together. Conversations are balanced, with equal contributions, lots of curiosity, interest and listening. The team values each other, and the unique contributions that each person makes are recognized.

If we know that belonging at work is consequential, and we know what it can look like, how can we develop it? As leaders it is important to create the opportunities for people within the team to have time together where relationships can form, trust can be built, shared connections can be made and recognized, and where this can be done in an informal way too. If we focus too much on work output all the time, we may lose the chances for people to informally connect. More formal time like team development days, where colleagues have the chance to interact in a different way, with a focus on interactions and team relationships, can also support this. It is also critical to think about ways in which to support hybrid or remote workers to feel included and that they belong, particularly when they might feel excluded from opportunities occurring within the team's physical space.

WAYS IN WHICH TO HELP HYBRID OR REMOTE WORKERS FEEL INCLUDED IN A TEAM OR ORGANIZATION

- The first step is to ask them what helps them to feel connected, as everyone is different and may value different things.

- Informal catch-up spaces can be helpful, including space for just remote workers to connect, and opportunities to catch up with people in the office too.

- Include a task/game at the start of a meeting, so that everyone contributes.

- Cameras on! Make sure that everyone has IT that is working, including cameras (and that their audio sounds okay), and that they stay on during the meeting.

- Check in with them before important meetings to see if there is anything that they particularly want to say/get across, and make sure that they have had the opportunity, or bring them into discussions.

- Perhaps create a 'meeting expectations' for video calls with your team, highlighting things such as different ways to contribute (e.g., raise a virtual hand, write in chat, use online resources such as polls).

- Use breakout spaces for smaller discussions.

- Invite them into discussions – ask for their input directly.

- Think about the communications you have with them – how might they differ from the communications you have with the rest of your team? Do you have informal space with them, too, to just check in?

- Make sure you have breaks in between meetings so you can check in and catch up.

- Recognize the potential impact on them of so much screen time and not as much informal catch-up in-person space. Some people will thrive on this; others will find it more difficult or will miss connecting with others. Think about their individual needs, and how these can be met within the work environment.

In later chapters within this book, we talk about other things at work that can lead to enhanced feelings of belonging, such as shared values and being part of the development and implementation of the team vision: seeing how your role fits into the bigger picture (Chapter 3), feeling trusted (Chapter 4), understanding and seeing your part in the team or organizational story (Chapter 8), and feeling psychologically safe (Chapter 9).

Coaching conversations

As we have been reflecting on in this chapter, one of the biggest elements of leadership is supporting the development of your team. When we are busy and trying to cope with lots of demands, it is easy to fall into a relationship with our team where we end up directing and giving advice most of the time. They come to us with a query, and we give them an answer and some direction. Sometimes this is absolutely the right thing to do, particularly in a crisis, when they might be looking for some clear direction and a steer or when a decision needs to be made quickly. However, most of the time, we can look at this another way, as an opportunity to support the development of knowledge, skills and confidence in our team, by coaching them to think about how to tackle a challenge or deal with a situation.

As discussed in the section 'Individual debriefs' earlier in this chapter, when team members are 'coached' rather than 'told', it can be empowering, can help them to develop their skills in decision making, can build their confidence, and can help them to recognize and draw on their individual strengths, knowledge and expertise. It can help them to feel more trusted by their leader (see Chapter 7 for a discussion on how powerful this can be). It also often supports them to find a solution to a problem that is a 'better fit', as when people give advice, they often do not have a full understanding of the context so there may be more challenges than they realize with the solution that they propose. It also gives an opportunity to support mastery, helping people to muddle through to find their own solutions, and through this process, recognize what they do well and create a real sense of achievement.

EXAMPLES OF QUESTIONS THAT COULD BE USED DURING COACHING CONVERSATIONS

- What is the challenge you are facing? What do you think could be underlying it? Or causing it? How did you come to that understanding?

- What do you really want? What would you like to change/develop? What would you do if you had no worries or fears, if no 'buts' existed?

- What would that look like? What would achieving this get you? Why is this particularly important for you, personally? Why is it important for you right now?

- What (or who) has been getting in the way? What is the underlying fear/worry? Or what is missing? How real are these fears or consequences to you? Have you got any personal barriers that might be holding you back?

- What could be other ways of seeing the situation?

- What would enable you to face/deal with that challenge?

- Have you been through similar challenges/situations before? What helped? Or, with hindsight, what would have made a difference?

- What is helping/supporting you right now? How is it helping? What has helped you to get to where you are so far?

- What options do you have? What else could you do?

- Who/what can help?

- What are your next steps? What is the first step that you need to take? What is a realistic step that you feel that you could commit to? What would you need to do this?

What a good coach looks like

Every person who has coaching conversations is going to do it a bit differently, and as we discuss in later chapters, one of the most important things in leadership is to be genuine, so although we will give some pointers in this chapter, it is also important to be yourself, and not just read out a list of questions.

We would recommend reflecting on who has been a good and encouraging coach to you, throughout your career, and what you liked about their approach. Through discussions with others, the following trends tend to arise:

Coaching characteristics

Characteristics that can be helpful	Characteristics that can be unhelpful
Is receptive and attentive to what they are hearing Stays curious – asks lots of follow-up questions so that they can fully understand the other person's perspective Picks out potential strengths from the person's narrative (and recognizes what they are already doing well), and names and is curious about these Summarizes and paraphrases what has been said, while checking out this understanding with the individual: *So, what I'm hearing is...* Notices and carefully names any non-verbal communication: e.g., *When you started to talk about X, you seemed angry? Was it bringing something up for you?* Acknowledges and is curious about any discrepancies, judgements or apparent conflicts in the person's account Draws distinctions: *When you say 'overwhelmed', is that within work, within a specific aspect of your role, or within life in general?* Helps the person to think in a critical way about their dominant thoughts and beliefs and to consider what might be underlying some of their behaviours and choices	Works through a 'checklist' of coaching questions without really listening to the person's answers Talks too much about themselves or their experience (takes over), particularly when it does not fit with the individual's own context 'Rescues' when they can see that the individual is feeling some discomfort; one of the challenges about this is that when someone is 'rescued', this can give the impression to the individual that the coach believes they are incapable of coping or of being able to come up with a solution and need someone else to step in Gives advice without really listening to what the challenges are Just sits within a reflection space, without supporting the person to move to action

Has an initial focus on understanding what the person wants out of the session, with an acknowledgement that this might change as a deeper understanding is created

Aims to identify any blockers or obstacles to the person achieving their goal, and helps them to identify potential solutions or ways forward

Believes that the person they are coaching can arrive at potential solutions themselves, and that their own role is as a guide to support the person to do this

By the end of the conversation, the person ideally has a deeper understanding of their situation or challenge, and has an idea of something they are going to consider further or an achievable next step

It's also useful to note that we sometimes find that there is a difference between how the person coaching thinks that a conversation has gone and how the person who was coached thinks it has gone. Occasionally, a coach may think that they had a productive, empowering conversation with someone, with the other person having left the room feeling dejected, overwhelmed or confused. It can therefore be helpful to make space for feedback on how the person found the session, what they found of benefit, whether it met their aims, or whether they would prefer a different approach. Getting regular feedback on your coaching style can be extremely beneficial in further developing your own leadership skills, and your relationship with your team.

When we provide supervision for others, we acknowledge that it is important to get 'supervision for ourselves about supervision'. The same thing applies with coaching. It is important to have a reflective space where you can discuss, consider and reflect on your experience of coaching others. There might be things or emotions that come up for us when facilitating the coaching, and we need to be aware of when we are being pulled to react in a particular way or being drawn to over-identify with the person we are coaching, for example. Supervision or reflective space around this can help us to develop greater self- and other-awareness, and can hone our coaching skills.

SELF-REFLECTION

- What drives, motivates and inspires you in work (or what has done so in the past)? How can you stay connected with this?

- Considering your team, how can you build autonomy, competence and relatedness?

- What might be some of the enablers or barriers to a sense of belonging for individuals in your team? How can you ensure that there is space for connection and building relationships through team interactions?

- What might you personally need to hold in mind when giving positive, negative and developmental feedback?

- How could you improve your coaching conversational skills?

- Reflect on people who have supported your leadership journey, and consider how they have supported or enabled you.

Summary

When we use psychological theory to develop our understanding of the motivations and drives of people we work with, we can consider how best to engage with, enable and bring healthy challenge to our teams. Supporting and developing those around us is a key, if not the most important, part of leadership, which creates cohesive, engaged and enthusiastic teams. Where we can 'lean into' discussions about performance and growth, and integrate this into part of our every-day practice, we can develop a team culture where each individual (and the team as a whole) is constantly developing, learning and improving their performance. When we can create a sense of safety, belonging and connection, this allows our colleagues to feel more able to take on challenges and be creative. To do this, we also need to create an environment where a growth mindset is nurtured, and it is okay to get things wrong at times. We discuss this further in Chapter 2, where we explore what innovation can look like in environments where it is okay to 'fail', and how we can enable our staff further by allowing them to think outside the box, take appropriate risks and overcome unnecessary barriers.

References and recommended reading

Allen, K.-A., Kern, M. L., Rozek, C. S., McInerney, D. M. and Slavich, G. M. (2021) 'Belonging: A review of conceptual issues, an integrative framework, and directions for future research.' *Australian Journal of Psychology 73*, 1, 87–102. doi: 10.1080/00049530.2021.1883409.

Carr, E. W., Reece, A., Kellerman, G. R. and Robichaux, A. (2019) 'Inclusion and belonging: The value of belonging at work.' *Harvard Business Review*, 16 December. https://hbr.org/2019/12/the-value-of-belonging-at-work

Deci, E. L., Olafsen, A. H. and Ryan, R. M. (2017) 'Self-determination theory in work organizations: The state of a science.' *Annual Review of Organizational Psychology and Organizational Behavior 4*, 19–43. https://psycnet.apa.org/record/2017-17803-002

Legault, L. (2017) 'Self-Determination Theory.' In V. Zeigler-Hill and T. K. Shackelford (eds) *Encyclopaedia of Personality and Individual Differences* (pp.4694–4702). Cham: Springer. doi: 10.1007/978-3-319-28099-8_1162-1.

Microsoft (2022) *Great Expectations: Making Hybrid Work Work*. Work Trend Index: Annual Report. www.microsoft.com/en-us/worklab/work-trend-index/great-expectations-making-hybrid-work-work

Scott, K. (2017) *Radical Candor: Be a Kick-Ass Boss Without Losing Your Humanity*. New York: St Martin's Press.

For further information on coaching skills:

Ashley-Timms, L. and Ashley-Timms, D. (2022) *The Answer Is a Question: The Missing Superpower That Changes Everything and Will Transform Your Impact as a Manager and Leader*. Norwich: TSO.

Jonsson, M. (2022) *The Complete Corporate Coaching Toolkit: The Quintessential Guide for 21st Century Business Coaches and Leaders* [Independently published].

Sternad, D. (2021) *Developing Coaching Skills: A Concise Introduction*. Moosburg, Austria: econcise Publishing.

CHAPTER 2

Enabling Others: Creativity, Innovation and Failure

In this chapter, we explore why it is important to try, try and try again, why in order to support your team to be truly creative and innovative, it is essential, as a leader, to build a culture where they can try things out and embrace the risk that things may not work out as hoped – a culture where failure is acknowledged and seen as part of the process of learning rather than ignored or hidden. Leaders need to be supporting their teams and organizations to constantly be adapting to an ever-changing context. It is therefore crucial to create environments where creativity and 'thinking outside the box' are supported and even celebrated.

Growth mindset

An important psychological term when discussing innovation and failure is a 'growth mindset'. As a leader, to be able to create psychologically responsive team environments that promote learning and growth, it is essential to understand this concept and how you can support it within your team's culture. Carol Dweck (a psychologist from Stanford University) first coined the term, which refers to an understanding that we learn through trial and error, and therefore failure is both inevitable and important (Dweck 2017). If we were to view failure as inherently negative, our goals and endeavour would be limited by our perceived need to avoid failure. We would essentially be limiting what we perceive as possible and worth taking a risk on, and restricting our opportunities to learn, develop and achieve. In fact, this 'fixed mindset' could lead us to set ourselves up for failure by restricting our own ability to engage in open learning. Alternatively, a growth mindset encourages us to accept the reality of failure as part of learning. When we can see the value of a growth mindset, this can help us to manage the difficult emotions that can come along with learning and failure. Setbacks and getting things wrong are seen as part of the process and can encourage us to try again. We may feel brave for trying something new, or even enjoy 'giving things a go'. However, if failure is viewed as a negative outcome, this can lead to feelings of shame, anxiety, frustration or upset.

As a psychologically responsive leader, as we consider within this and future chapters, it is important to be able to show some fallibility and vulnerability. We will not always have the answers, and it is helpful to model to your team that it is okay to not know sometimes and to ask for help. Therefore, the promotion of a growth mindset within your team is important for ongoing learning and being able to manage failure and setbacks well.

What is innovation?

When we are able to develop team and organizational cultures that foster a growth mindset, and are open to learning and growth, then we are able to consider how we can be more creative and innovative. Innovation is a process of finding a radically different approach or solution, something that has not been tried before. In the areas in which we work, we often focus on replicating what we know is evidence-based or already known as good practice – if we want to do something well, we might research what has worked well in that area before. Alternatively, we might think about how we can be creative with what we have got, such as adapting an approach or way of working. However, sometimes there might be an opportunity to truly try out something completely new. Within commercial settings, innovation is key to staying competitive and driving performance and growth.

One of the dangers that we often see in health, social care and education is people continuing to do things because 'that is the way that they have always been done'. This can be ways of working, systems or practices. When the contexts and problems we are facing are constantly changing, both in our society and within our work, as humans we can crave certainty and stability. This can mean that we stick to what we know so that we feel safer. However, innovation may be needed when we are facing new challenges, the old practices are no longer working, or maybe we just want to experiment to see if we can improve our work to make it more effective or efficient.

What can get in the way of innovation?

Peter Skillman was a designer and engineer who undertook some experiments to explore how different groups (from children in nursery to business students at university) would approach an innovation task (as described by Coyle (2019)). He asked them to build the tallest freestanding tower that would support the weight of a marshmallow using a few items (dried spaghetti, masking tape and string).[1] He found that the business students typically started by discussing the task, reflecting on it in a strategic manner and considering the different materials. They came up with a few potential solutions, and thought through the pros and cons of each, before choosing which to take forward. They then decided who would do what part of the build. However, the nursery children took a completely different approach. They hardly talked, but instead shouted out a few comments about what they were doing while standing close to each other. They picked up materials and tried things out straight away, then gave up quickly when it did not work, and tried something else. Who do you think won the task? It was the nursery children, whose towers were 26 inches tall on average, compared to the business students' towers that were less than 10 inches tall. But why was this?

---

1   An excerpt about the marshmallow experiment is available at: https://daniel-coyle.com/excerpt-culture-code

Skillman proposed that this result was likely due to the business students trying to use their prior learning and assumptions and apply them to the problem, despite the problem being a new situation for them. Some parts of the problem may have seemed quite familiar, having used some items previously (e.g., masking tape), and potentially having built towers of some kind in the past. But putting these elements together made the problem unique and new. For example, they might not have realized that the marshmallow was quite a heavy weight for a fragile tower of uncooked spaghetti to hold. However, the nursery children picked up these new rules quite quickly as they 'had a go', tested out any potential assumptions, experimented quickly, failed, and thus learned about the properties of the items. If something did not work, they tried something else. This is using more spatial and creative right hemisphere brain functioning. The business students, however, tended to try to stick to their original, carefully thought-out idea, just making tweaks rather than a full new design when things failed. This is using more logical left hemisphere brain functioning. The latter is something that can often happen in workplaces – sticking with an original idea even when it is clearly not working (as so much has been invested in it already) rather than deciding to stop and try something else.

This means that sometimes the way that we work and what we prioritize (e.g., planning, careful consideration of the pros and cons, using prior assumptions and tweaking what we are doing rather than a full redesign) can get in the way of us finding the best solution for a novel problem that we encounter.

When we are faced with a challenge, it may be helpful to consider whether this is a good opportunity for innovation, or a time for drawing on existing knowledge.

In order to be truly innovative, as leaders and within our organizational culture, we need to be able to take risks and potentially fail, fail and fail again, before we finally find the best solution. Therefore, failure is an essential part of leadership and the innovation process that is central to any healthy organization.

The term 'failure' tends to have a negative connotation; however, when we view it as a core part of the learning process, it is an inevitable outcome of positive endeavour. If we are going to try things and push ourselves within our organization, and would like our teams to feel that they are comfortable doing the same, then we are sometimes going to fail.

Different types of failure

We now explore some different types of failure so that you can see how you, as a psychologically responsive leader, can understand and make the most out of failure and view it as an opportunity for learning wherever possible.

There are lots of different types of failure, including:

- *Avoidable or preventable failure (also known as 'basic' failure):* This is when an organization might seem to be doing okay and then something suddenly goes very wrong. For example, where there were people within an organization who knew about the underlying challenges that were factors in an incident but who did not feel able to speak up (perhaps due to a lack of psychological safety; see Chapter 9), or a person made an avoidable error as they were distracted, unprepared or not taking care.

- *Sitting in failure:* When we are doing something that we know is not working, but we continue to do the same thing despite knowing it will not work (perhaps because it is what we have always done, or we feel restricted by the boundaries of our team or role, or we feel unable to try something different).

- *Complex failure:* When something goes wrong that we were not expecting, from a complex and novel set of circumstances (which may have been interconnected, so it can be more difficult to find an exact cause), which gives us the opportunity to create a better understanding of what went wrong and to learn from this.

- *Intelligent failure:* As described by Edmondson (2023), this is when we allow ourselves to try out new things, test a hypothesis, be creative and innovative or try to find the best solution to a problem. This can support us to learn quickly, innovate effectively, experiment, discuss openly and find the best solutions. Sitkin (1992) suggests that intelligence failures are smaller experiments, which are based on some prior learning, where no unnecessary harm has been caused, and that are purposeful as they aim to promote learning and understanding in a specific area.

Obviously within our work in health, social care and education, there are times when it is not appropriate to 'fail', such as in our care for the people we support. However, if we, as leaders, can create environments where it is okay to be creative and to try new things out, then we can find even better solutions for our organizations and those we support, rather than doing the same thing we have always done where it might not be working.

How to create services where innovation and failure are valued

If we want to truly innovate as leaders or within our teams, the first step is often to define what the problem is – what are we trying to 'solve' and what are the challenges that we are facing? To do this, we might want to talk to different stakeholders about their perspective of the problem and how they understand it.

There are lots of areas where we can be creative or innovative, for example:

- Creating a new product

- Setting up a new process or system – either internal (with our own team) or external

- Considering how we build our network/create connections with others
- Thinking about how we engage with those we are working with/serving
- Thinking about what our brand looks like, and how we articulate it
- Considering how we promote our service
- Thinking about how we evaluate our service/get feedback
- Setting up a system to monitor outcomes in our service.

The next step is to generate lots of potential ideas or solutions, which can then be tested out. It is important at this stage to consider all ideas that are generated, rather than choosing one initially and then sticking with it to the end, as this leads us to be less flexible. If we want to be truly innovative at this stage, we should start this process recognizing that we do not know what the best solution will look like so that we can be open to all ideas. Subsequently, we can go through a 'funnelling' process, where ideas are trialled out and compete against each other to see which ones outcompete the others. Eventually, perhaps after several 'rounds' of trying out the different ideas, one will become the more obvious best solution.

An example of how the NHS has been attempting to innovate, through generating lots of ideas and pitting them against each other, is the Solving Together online conversation. This project focuses on gaining a range of stakeholder perspectives, learning and ideas on how they can improve waiting times and make services more accessible.

Solving Together: An online conversation about reducing waiting times for children and young people's mental health services

Bev Matthews, Assistant Director of Programmes (Collaboration) at NHS England, has been leading an innovative project named Solving Together. For the first time, the NHS launched a month-long online conversation on children and young people's community mental health, with a focus on gathering ideas about how they could improve waiting times and make services more accessible. Using a crowdsourcing approach, they invited partners involved in the children and young people's community mental health pathway, professionals, children and young people, their families and support networks to have a say about this critical issue, with a focus on gathering ideas and examples of what works, and building a community of people who can make change happen to improve NHS services. Several big ideas, created by filtering the activity on the platform, will be generated, and tested with teams across the country.[2]

Some approaches to innovation draw from intrapersonal psychology (considering an individual's internal model of learning, such as a growth mindset) and interpersonal psychology (such as building an empathic understanding of the 'client', their perspectives and their needs). For example, Google's Creative Skills for Innovation Lab (CSI:Lab) has identified three 'creative forces' that it uses when cultivating creativity and innovation in teams:

- *Empathy:* Taking time to really understand the perspective, needs and motivations of the user of the service or product. This helps to ensure that the end product is meaningful and useful to the person that it is intended to serve. This can be done by consulting with key stakeholders and asking curious questions, or in creative ways such as drawing out, or imagining, the potential impact on different people within the process.

- *Multiscale thinking:* Creating many ideas initially, with a focus on quantity rather than quality at first. Google has found that smaller groups can often be best to generate ideas and remain productive in this. Google also asks teams to think

---

2   See www.england.nhs.uk/blog/solvingtogether-how-can-we-recover-planned-and-elective-care-in-the-nhs

'audaciously' to come up with ideas that are 'ten times' better than what is currently in place, which can help them to think creatively without the usual barriers in place.

- *Experiment:* Try out the ideas, test and gather real-life data. This might be, for example, through a small pilot project. Following this, see what they can learn, and if they want to continue with the project, or stop completely, or make some tweaks.

SOME TIPS FOR INNOVATION

- See intelligent failure as an opportunity for learning and experimenting.

- Consider all ideas and potential solutions equally at first – there are no 'bad' ideas.

- Encourage everyone to contribute, and discuss and consider ideas (including half-baked ones).

- Filter and funnel quickly – try things out, experiment and discard the things that do not work. Try not to become too attached to one idea at the start, as this can get in the way of potentially finding the best solution.

Systems thinking and innovation

Systems thinking is a school of psychology that recognizes the interactive, dynamic nature of interpersonal groups. The group could be anything from a family structure to a society. This psychological theory explores how different parts of the system work together to ensure the overall stability and balance of the group. It recognizes that what occurs within one part of the system will have a knock-on effect and inherently impact the other parts of the system. This therefore highlights the importance of you, as leaders, bringing together stakeholders to think psychologically and collaboratively about the system as a whole, the roles and impacts of their individual parts, and how these interact together. When focusing on innovation, systems thinking invites leaders to encourage stakeholders from a range of sectors or organizations to come together to focus collaboratively on a societal challenge and innovate together around this.

When we apply systems thinking we start by creating a shared understanding of what the challenge or problem is, by exploring and truly listening to the needs and perspectives of all stakeholders (e.g., young people, parents/carers, staff, managers, wider systems, commissioners, other services involved) – how does this issue affect them? How do they understand it? What is their context? Within psychology, we often use the term 'systemic formulation', which aims to bring together different perspectives and narratives to create a more coherent, whole and shared understanding of a system and associated dynamics. When we create this formulation, it then allows a deeper shared understanding for everyone involved, and ensures that as leaders and members of the organization or team we hold different accounts in mind at all stages of the process, and that the end result will hopefully talk to the needs of everyone affected. The leader then encourages a discussion around potential ideas and novel solutions, and pulls together an action plan, which often includes aligned actions across the group to enable a bigger impact. Then the group explores further, or pilots one or a few ideas (usually starting small). Outcomes measurement is embedded in the process, with the opportunity for all stakeholders to give feedback. If the proposed solution is successful, tweaks based on the feedback can be made, and then it could be rolled out further.

SELF-REFLECTION

- If you had the opportunity to innovate collaboratively around a shared challenge or problem, what would that be?

- Who would be the key stakeholders who would need to be

involved? And/or who might you want to bring on board/ who could you consult with?

- How would you start this process? What would your first step be?

Here is an example of where systems thinking has been applied by leaders within a locality through multiple service providers working collaboratively around a shared issue (trauma-informed care). The coalition that formed developed a shared understanding to enable them to identify key objectives needed to deliver their services within a trauma-informed manner bespoke to their community.

The West Midlands Trauma Informed Coalition: Systems thinking

In 2021, the West Midlands Combined Authority (WMCA) commissioned a piece of research called 'Punishing abuse' by Dr Alex Chard, which highlighted the systemic need to address trauma and adversity within the region. This piece of work became a driver for establishing the West Midlands Trauma Informed Coalition (commissioned by the WMCA, Office of the Police and Crime Commissioner and Barnardo's). A group of senior leaders came together to collaborate around the findings of this report (representing policing, the fire service, probation, social care, local authorities, health, education, third sector and faith-based organizations). Initially there were around 30 leaders, and a design sprint was undertaken to ascertain the best collaborative evidence base from both research and practice, to see where the gaps were, and what was needed to collectively develop and embed a region-wide vision and programme around trauma-informed practice.

Consultation was undertaken with the different leaders and wider services, to gain a real understanding of the challenges that the different areas were facing. Some of the key learnings from the project were around the use of language and terminology, and there was a real consensus within the group about how language needed to be understandable, and how there needed to be clarity around what was meant by 'trauma-informed'. The group further recognized that rather than focusing solely on adverse childhood experiences (ACEs), they wanted to recognize the impact of trauma, with an emphasis on traumatic stress, and an acknowledgement of collective trauma, organizational trauma, secondary traumas and intergenerational trauma. It was also agreed that cultural sensitivity and supporting those with lived experience of trauma was essential, so these considerations became an integral part of the strategy in all areas. This led to a regional definition of trauma-informed practice being created to represent the unique context of the West Midlands. It was also recognized that there needed to be some clear guidance around funding, to support commissioners to understand what they were commissioning and what should be considered at each stage to ensure high-quality provision that considered the cultural context of the West Midlands.

As momentum started to build, it was recognized that someone needed to coordinate this effort going forward. Barnardo's was then commissioned to oversee the work and drive the strategic actions forward through Lucy Cavell (Senior Trauma-Informed Practitioner).

Four key strategic deliverables were identified and commissioned on behalf of the coalition:

- *Creation of an online community of practice:* An online space for professionals in the West Midlands to share reflections, best practice and knowledge, to post and access resources, listen to guest speakers, and to enable learning together. Forums are also available where practitioners from a range of organizations can share dilemmas, feeling stuck and key issues, and learn from each other. Over 200 professionals are now registered on this platform.

- *Workforce Learning and Development Framework:* A framework that includes clear benchmarks and expectations for different levels of understanding and skills, and clear definitions around what it means to be 'trauma aware', 'trauma informed' and 'trauma responsive' in the West Midlands.

- *Social cost and benefit analysis (reducing systemic trauma, developing systemic resilience):* Analysis to provide critical evidence to support the financial rationale for trauma-informed practice. It was recognized that the impacts of trauma-informed provision can be difficult to measure as they are wide ranging, so by collating information about the financial impact overall, this can support services to argue for the need for a more trauma-informed approach in their organization.

- *Commissioning Framework:* To support commissioners and funding bodies to consider the whole commissioning process from a trauma-informed perspective, including scoping and strategic needs assessments, the tender process, contracting arrangements, contract management and how provision can be evaluated and sustainable, alongside their own reflective practice and knowledge development.

Within the Workforce Learning and Development Framework group, there was initially a reference group of approximately 35 members. Some qualitative interviews were undertaken to find out the perspectives and views from each sector, which led to the identification of key themes. Where there appeared to be conflicting views or challenges, further conversations were had to gain a greater understanding of the differences and potential collective ways forward. The frameworks (both Learning and Development, and Commissioning) then went out for public consultation – an online survey was sent to the wider coalition, with permission for them to send it out to capture the perspectives of wider stakeholders and people the organizations were supporting. In total around 100 people were consulted. This survey gave the opportunity to comment on the use of terminology and language, the design of the frameworks, how accessible they felt, and what 'good' would look and feel like in terms of commissioning.

Lucy has reflected on how the consultation with the different sectors has helped to develop her own awareness of how important it is to take time to fully understand the concepts from all perspectives – for example, taking time to really wrestle out what the terms mean to different organizations (e.g., trauma aware/ trauma informed) and what might be included at each level. It has also been helpful to consider how different professionals will bring their own filters to their work, based on their context and the team they work in.

When writing a document from your own perspective, it will likely speak to the context that you write from, but may miss the perspectives, understandings and filters of others. For example, when writing a document around trauma-informed practice, someone working predominantly within residential care may apply a 'complex trauma' lens. However, the document may then not be as useful for those working within services where post-traumatic stress is the predominant presentation, or for organizations where there has been a single major incident affecting a community. Therefore, it is important when doing this type of work to truly consult with a wide range of organizations and communities that you are trying to serve, to ensure that your work is speaking in tones that resonate and are relevant for everyone involved.

The work therefore identified key themes that were relevant across all the organizations and areas and that allowed for autonomy for people to be creative and innovative in how to apply these within their own contexts. The work also recognized and honoured the good practice that had gone before, or that was still being carried out within organizations, and it was hoped that the frameworks would enhance this further.

The work undertaken so far is owned by everyone who has been involved in the coalition. Although Barnardo's coordinates this work, it has shared ownership, with the people involved both holding each other to account and being each other's biggest cheerleaders. There are now over 180 members in the coalition, representing public and third sector organizations (from mid to executive levels) across the West Midlands. Although the members are often busy leaders, many of them are really engaged in the coalition work and see the benefit. The Strategic Governance Group are working hard (on behalf of the wider group) to try to bridge any gaps, to ensure that under-represented groups are included (such as faith-based organizations), and to consider how they can better make links with these communities. The next steps for the coalition are to continue to strengthen relationships and support organizations to really embed trauma-informed practice and the frameworks created so far.

This example gives a detailed account of what systems thinking can look like in practice. It shows the importance of you, as a leader, truly consulting with those who are likely to be impacted by new service developments, so that their perspectives and experiences are understood, to ensure that any decisions made will take into account the needs of all involved. There is a danger that we, as leaders, instead act on assumptions of the needs of the different parties, rather than taking the time to listen and understand, leading to an outcome that does not fit the needs of the community. As Google's CSI:Lab highlighted, taking the time to empathize and understand the perspectives, needs and motivations of the people it will impact is an essential element of innovating well. In addition, this example from the West Midlands highlights the powerful, meaningful and impactful changes that can occur when systems come together to think, build understanding and innovate.

Summary

Within this chapter, we have considered how you, as a leader, can shape the mindset of your team, from one that might be fixed, fearful and reluctant to take risks to one that feels safer, understands failure as an inherent part of endeavour, and is more creative and innovative. When we are thinking systemically, this allows us to drive greater change. We can bring psychological systemic thinking to build shared understanding so that the outcomes consider the needs of all involved, therefore making the outcomes more likely to be successful and meaningful. Where we, as leaders, can bring together a group, team or organization to think and reflect together, this can allow us to create shared meaning, vision and purpose. We will explore this further in the next chapter.

References and recommended reading

Coyle, D. (2019) *The Culture Code: The Secrets of Highly Successful Groups.* New York: Random House Business.

Dweck, C. (2017) *Mindset: Changing the Way You Think to Fulfil Your Potential.* New York: Robinson.

Edmondson, A. (2023) *The Right Kind of Wrong: Why Learning to Fail Can Teach Us to Thrive.* London: Cornerstone Press.

Pferdt, F. G. (2020) 'Design thinking in 3 steps: How to build a culture of innovation.' Think with Google, February. www.thinkwithgoogle.com/intl/en-emea/future-of-marketing/creativity/design-thinking-principles

Sitkin, S. B. (1992) 'Learning through failure: The strategy of small losses.' *Research in Organizational Behavior 14*, 231–266.

CHAPTER 3

Vision and Values

Why do we do what we do? What keeps us grounded and willing to get up in the morning? How does this contribute to the bigger picture and where we are wanting our organizations to head as leaders? Human beings have an innate need for meaningful connection with others, a sense of belonging and a sense of purpose, and these are inherently linked to our wellbeing. The psychological research and literature around resilience also highlights 'purpose' as a key factor that can help individuals and groups to survive and find meaning and growth through challenging experiences. This applies to us both in our personal and our professional lives. Therefore, it is important to embrace this psychological knowledge in order to get the best from ourselves as leaders, and so from our colleagues and our organizations. This psychological knowledge can be applied to us as individual leaders, but it can also be applied to us as groups and teams, and at a societal or cultural level.

Within this chapter we explore how as leaders we can build a sense of meaningful connection within our teams, and a clear sense of purpose along with a strategic plan to help us to achieve our purpose and experience success. We draw on our knowledge of acceptance and commitment therapy (ACT) to support a deeper understanding of, and connection to, values that can enhance our development as leaders. We explore the importance of our 'why' (purpose), and the need for clarity around our vision and values as well as those of our team or organization. We discuss a range of ways in which to develop these, to operationalize and embed them within a service.

Organizational mission, vision and values

You have probably seen many team and organizational visions, mission statements and values within your career. These statements can often use similar language, so there can be a lot of overlap and a sense of familiarity. They are often stated on organizational websites when talking about the ethos of the organization, or displayed as you enter a building. However, we often find when talking to teams that although they might be aware that these visions or values exist, they do not really know how they came about, or what their underlying meaning is. In fact, we have sometimes had debates in teams where individuals have completely different understandings of mission or values statements, due to the language used (see Chapter 5). When asked what these might look like in day-to-day practice, staff can often struggle to articulate this, or simply say that they do not know. This is common and perhaps indicative of instances when a big piece of work may have been completed in defining the mission, vision and values, but then, over time, the meaning can be lost if it is not truly embedded. If it does not remain meaningful to the teams working within the service or for those that the organization serves, then the worth of the mission, vision and values work is lost.

The importance of having an embedded mission, vision and values

Having a considered and clear mission statement (purpose), vision statement and identified core values in a team or organization informs the goal, direction, strategy and planning of the team. This encourages a clear and positive mindset within a team, which is likely to lead to greater achievement and success. A sense of achievement reinforces a team's sense of agency and capability, which leads to improved wellbeing. It provides a framework and allows the team to hold a bigger picture of their desired destination and the meaning of the goals for themselves and their team, without becoming too narrowly focused on the day-to-day actions of their work. Clarity around a team's purpose, vision and values helps the leader, and team, to stay on track when challenging times arise or choices need to be made. It helps the leader to communicate what is important, what they are hoping to achieve, and why. It also helps the leader to communicate concisely, both internally and externally, what their aims and purpose are, which allows employees, investors and customers to 'buy in' to the team's purpose and can set the organization apart from the competition. It can also attract people to want to come to work within the team, and want to stay, if they align with the team's values or purpose, and they can see how they are evident in the organization's work. Having a clear purpose, vision and values informs the team's strategy and the evaluation and monitoring of the team's work – are *they* working towards *their* purpose and vision and what is important to the team?

In fact, without a clear vision and values it can be difficult to ensure everyone is on board with and working towards the same purpose. Different assumptions and expectations may lead to team members, or teams within an organization, working at odds with one another, even if unintentionally. Having a shared purpose can help the team to build better relationships with one another and help them to negotiate differences and challenges. But once the team knows what their purpose, vision and values are, they still need to operationalize them and ensure that they are held in mind and they are working with them and towards them, reviewing and evaluating their progress along the way.

The purpose (or mission), vision and values of an organization both help to tell the story of the organization and shape its story. As human beings we make sense of life, the world and our experience in the form of stories (as discussed in more depth in Chapter 8), so the stories we create and share about our organization, and that will also shape our organization, are vitally important.

Simon Sinek's Golden Circle: Start with the 'why?'

Simon Sinek is a leadership guru who devised the Golden Circle (2011) to explain how an organization communicates, internally and externally, its purpose, cause or belief (why?), and how the organization achieves this (what?). Sinek argues that we truly inspire our employees, colleagues and clients by clearly articulating our purpose – why we do what we do. This helps individuals to understand what we are trying to achieve, what we are passionate about and the story behind what we do as an organization. People buy into this story and purpose more than the product, Sinek argues. So, while many leaders and organizations start from outside the Golden Circle and work in, Sinek states that inspiring leaders work from the inside out, and 'Start with the why'. The 'why?' in Sinek's Golden Circle relates to our purpose (our mission statement) and our values.

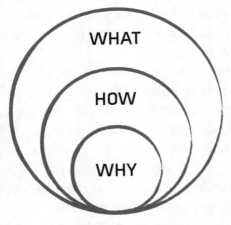

Sinek's Golden Circle theory

- *Why:* Why does your particular team or organization exist? What is the organization's purpose or underlying cause?

- *How:* How do you, as a team or organization, meet your 'why?' or purpose?

- *What:* What exactly do you do in your organization day to day that underlies your 'how?'?

Our how and what may change, but our why or purpose usually stays the same, so it is the most important factor in our organizational story and something we should be very clear about.

Here is an example of what our Golden Circle looks like for our work as clinical psychologists. We also give you guidance on how to create your own Golden Circle.

USING SINEK'S GOLDEN CIRCLE TO THINK ABOUT OUR WORK AS CLINICAL PSYCHOLOGISTS

- *Why?* Help improve the wellbeing of children, young people and families.

- *How?* Help other professionals to bring psychological thinking to their work; think systemically and have an impact at different levels of the system; be curious and prepared to challenge; seek new opportunities for work.

- *What?* Provide psychological consultation and training to professionals, co-create psychologically responsive frameworks for organizations, produce podcasts and articles and books, and provide therapy to children, young people and families.

Taking time as a team or senior leadership team, or the wider team, to think through carefully the three elements of the Golden Circle can help a team to have a shared and focused understanding of their goals and how the team intends to achieve these goals. Completing this task well can be a good first step in informing the organization's vision and strategy.

TEAM TASK: WHAT IS YOUR WHY?

Ask your team as individuals to answer the following questions, and then ask them to discuss the questions in pairs, being curious about their partner's thoughts and perspectives:

- Why do we do what we do?

- Why does this specific team or organization need to exist?

- Who do we serve?

- What impact do we want to have?

- What is our ultimate goal?

Depending on numbers, the pairs can feed back their thoughts or they can join with another pair to make a group of four to discuss their thoughts, before feeding back to the team. Once this information is collated, the key aspects of the team's purpose can start to take shape and be agreed on.

Writing a mission statement

Once we have defined our team/organization's purpose, we are able to articulate this as leaders and within the organization in a clear and concise mission statement. If you are composing this, focus on what is important to the organization and be brief, informative and clear, focusing on the goal of the organization and the people it is serving, avoiding complicated language and cliches.

Individual and team values

Intrinsically related to a team's purpose is its values. A team's values are its core principles and philosophical ideas that shape its goals, so it is often helpful to consider the team's values and purpose together. The team's values also inform and guide its decision making and behaviour, and therefore shape the culture of a team. They inform the standards that the team members set for themselves and against which their actions can be assessed, as individuals and as a group.

Taking time to think about the values that are important to us and how we want to live those values as leaders, and as teams, in our work, relationships and leisure time is extremely helpful to us, as individuals, in finding meaning in our lives, relationships and work. The same can be said for the life of any team or organization.

Defining values

Values are our beliefs and principles that are important to us person-ally. They shape our personal goals and achievements, and inform what is meaningful to us in life in terms of our relationships, our work, the way we spend time outside work and how we want to live our lives day to day. Our values help determine our goals and what we want to achieve (purpose) and how we want to live our lives (vision), and help guide us through difficult times. Our values help us to make decisions when we are faced with challenges, and guide us in devising new plans and direction of travel, helping us to find meaning in our work, even through difficult times, which helps us to be more psychologically fulfilled and resilient.

Members of a team will have different personal values, although often there will be some shared values associated with the work. Often individuals may use slightly different words to describe a similar value. For example, I may say honesty and empathy are important values to me, whereas my colleague may say integrity and caring are important to them. When we talk about these values with one another, we may find that we are valuing the same thing with slightly different words to describe what is important to us. Alternatively, you may have two colleagues who use the same language to describe a value that is important to them, but when this is explored further, this term may have different meanings for them. For example, for one person creativity may mean using art, drama or music within their work, whereas for another, it may mean allowing themselves to be innovative and to think 'outside the box'.

Taking time to reflect on individual values and what they mean for each person, and reflecting on those that the team members share, can really help individuals to feel understood, develop relationships and a sense of belonging between team members and, of course, help define their shared purpose. Values and purpose are not the same thing, but they are intrinsically related – for example, I may hold a value of kindness and helping others and my purpose in work may be to improve the lives of people.

Patrick Hackett, Registrar, Secretary and Chief Operating Officer, University of Manchester: Creating and embedding shared values

Our shared values help us to shape and strive to achieve our vision and strategy. Determining these values has been a collaborative and painstaking process across our university community of over 12,000 staff (and 45,000 students). When we renewed our strategy in 2020, more than 4000 staff engaged directly in the process of arriving at our six shared values. It was a long and demanding process in a large and complex organization, but it was very worthwhile and actually really enjoyable. The process got all sorts of wonderful conversations going in our different teams right around the university and that, in itself, rejuvenated us, not just in being clear about defining our shared values, but also in engaging with each other outside of the day-to-day urgent priorities that we can find all-consuming at times. We wanted to make the exercise itself meaningful for our people and for everyone to feel connected to the values, winning 'hearts and minds'.

Shared values cannot be forced on an organization. People have to be party to determining them and believe in them, so the upfront work is really crucial. We used a mixture of survey and small focus groups from different constituencies across our very diverse community. So, it was incredibly important that we were able to have representatives from all our community to participates in loads and loads of small focus groups. And then we brought larger groups together and we started feeding some of the information back to them and getting more detail, narrowing the values down and discussing what they meant together. Eventually, after many months of consultation, we were able to sign them off, along with our new university strategy, through our board.

If we have done the work well from the outset, hopefully most people will recognize one or more of the values that's particularly important to them. But, at a practical level, we now, through our professional development review process, have very clear sections to talk about our values and to ask ourselves through that process, 'What does this value mean?' and' What are we doing to operationalize it and to live up to each of those values?' We reflect at the annual review on how we are succeeding at living these values, where we have fallen down, and ask ourselves, 'What are we going to do differently next year?' That is probably the single most important thing that we've done to embed the values and bring them to life.

TEAM TASK: FOCUSING ON TEAM VALUES

For this task, you can use the list of values in the Appendix as a starting point or create your own. Initially, ask each team member to select up to six values that resonate with them personally about the work of the team, what is particularly important to the team, and how they would want to work together. It can be useful to ask them to consider:

- What do we stand for as a team?

- What is particularly important to us?

- What behaviours or principles do we value the most?

- What values might we need to hold in mind in order to achieve our purpose?

Once each person has identified their six values, it can be helpful to ask them to discuss the chosen values with a partner to deepen their understandings as to why they have chosen these particular values, and why they might be important to the team.

For the next step, ask each person to read out their six values, and make a note of them to identify which are the most shared values among the team. Then determine if there are values that are very similar but using different language that can be combined to represent one shared value of the team.

The aim of the task is not for everyone to agree. Some variation in values and perspectives is good. However, it is likely that there will be a few key values that are more widely shared by the team and that are connected to the team's work and align with the organization's ethos. For example, a design or creative team may well have common values such as innovation, bravery and passion, with several other values that differ between colleagues.

As a next step, start to talk through each of the common values to gain a greater understanding of what these might mean, and why they might be important to individuals within the team and the team as a group.

These most shared values that inform the purpose of the team's work may then be used as team values.

Writing a values statement

Having decided on the team/organizational values, these can be used to write a value statement. This can either be a short phrase or simply two or three words that are clear, memorable and actionable. The words should be fitting to the team over the long term rather than just for the short term. Once the purpose and values have been identified, these shape the vision and more detailed strategy.

Operationalizing values: bringing them to life

We have now identified our team values, but how can we, as leaders, make them meaningful and embed them within our day-to-day practice? Thinking about what these values mean in terms of our behaviours, habits and rituals really helps us to bring the values to life, helping us to *live our values* rather than simply naming them.

TEAM TASK: OPERATIONALIZING TEAM VALUES

Make sure that everyone relevant can attend the session – this is a great one to do with the whole team, as it is an opportunity for the team to take ownership of the values and the ways in which they want to work in line with them.

The facilitator (perhaps yourself) writes each value on the top of a sheet of flipchart paper. They ask the team, 'If we were to really live this value in our team, what would it look like? What would we and others see? What would be the same or different from what we are doing now?'

The first part of this task is individual. Each person is asked to write down suggestions (one per sticky note) of which (observable) behaviours they feel would fit with each value, and then to place their sticky notes on the relevant flipchart sheet. It is worth giving a bit of time to do this properly, so that people truly have time to think and reflect on each value and what it would look like in practice.

The team then splits up into small groups, and each chooses a value. Each group takes the flipchart paper (with suggestions attached) for that value and takes some time reading the suggestions through to get a greater understanding of the team's thinking in this area, and to look for any common themes in the suggested behaviours. Through discussion and debate, the small group then decides a core group of observable behaviours that link with that value that they feel could be put into place by the team. Once this has been completed for all the values, each team feeds back their value and proposed behaviours for further discussion and feedback, so that the team can reach an agreement.

Following this, it can then be useful to have a reference document with each value – what it means to the group (how they would define it), and what it looks like in practice within the team or organization (the observable behaviours).

As leaders, there are actions we can take to ensure our team values are understood and shape our work. Taking the time to discover collaboratively and articulate our team values is the first step. We then need to ensure the values are visible in the workspace, in documentation, on the website, and within communication, induction and recruitment processes. We can consider ways to hold them in mind when making decisions and at regular intervals during team discussions. Team days can be a good opportunity for the team to assess whether the team values are being fully embedded within the service and are present during day-to-day practice. We may also want to continue to consider whether these values hold meaning for colleagues in their work, rather than simply being words. Are there actions that we can take to allow us to be more aligned with our values day to day?

Reflection on values

Acceptance and commitment therapy (ACT) is an intervention that can support us to identify our core values, so that we can work out how to live and work in a way that is truly meaningful and fulfilling to us. This supports our psychological wellbeing and ability to manage challenging aspects of life. ACT can also be applied to groups and teams. When we use ACT with teams, it can also help us to start to consider and recognize some of the barriers and challenges that might be holding us (or our team or organization) back from working in a values-based way, and to think about how we can behave in a way that helps us to move closer to and align more with our core values over time.

TEAM TASK/SELF-REFLECTION: MAPPING OUT OUR VALUES

This reflection activity can be used either by individuals or with teams, to have space to reflect on some of the challenges you (or your team) face, and to create intentions and actions to move towards your (or your team's) desired values. To do this exercise, it can be useful to draw out the boxes on a whiteboard or big piece of paper and talk through the different areas and questions as a team.

We would recommend starting with 'Internal – towards' (your values as a group), and then moving to 'Internal – away'. The third box, 'External – away', can then encourage a discussion about what happens when the 'Internal – away' sabotaging thoughts, emotions or memories get in the way, and how this might lead the team to behave or act. Then the final box, 'External – towards', can lead to a discussion about how to move towards action: 'How can we behave in a way that is closer to our values?'

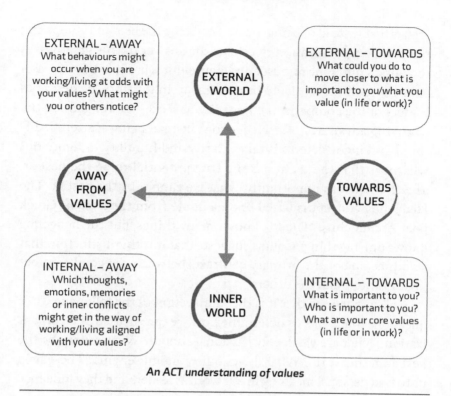

EXTERNAL – AWAY
What behaviours might occur when you are working/living at odds with your values? What might you or others notice?

EXTERNAL WORLD

EXTERNAL – TOWARDS
What could you do to move closer to what is important to you/what you value (in life or work)?

AWAY FROM VALUES

TOWARDS VALUES

INTERNAL – AWAY
Which thoughts, emotions, memories or inner conflicts might get in the way of working/living aligned with your values?

INNER WORLD

INTERNAL – TOWARDS
What is important to you? Who is important to you? What are your core values (in life or in work)?

An ACT understanding of values

Whenever we do a reflection exercise with a team, it can also be helpful to consider 'How can we now put this into practice?' to make sure that rather than just reflecting on the challenges, we are also thinking about how we can make positive changes in our work or our team and creating an action plan around this. We tend to find that teams who do lots of reflection (which we really like as psychologists), but without moving to action, can end up feeling hopeless, powerless and stuck, rather than energized with a sense that the team has a plan to take things forward.

The Hedgehog Concept

The Hedgehog Concept, articulated by the American business consultant Jim Collins (2024), shows how a company or person can achieve 'greatness' in business by adopting a certain psychological mindset and asking themselves three specific questions. Collins argues that instead of being focused on being the best and comparing our team or organization to others, the answer to true greatness is to adopt a different mindset and figure out what it is that we, as a team, have the potential to be the best at. In his story, he describes leaders of the comparison companies as 'Foxes', never gaining the clarifying advantage of a 'Hedgehog', instead being scattered, diffused and inconsistent. It takes clarity and humility to figure out what it is that the team has the true potential to be the best at, as well as, just as importantly, what we cannot be the best at. The Hedgehog concept is based upon a quote from the ancient Greek poet Archilochus: 'The fox knows many things, but the hedgehog knows one big thing.' Collins suggests that it is this distinction that stands as one of the primary contrasts between the good-to-great organizations and the others.

Collins suggests that it is the intersection of the following three questions that helps us determine how we can succeed as an organization: What are we deeply passionate about? What can we be the best at in the world? What drives our economic engine? These help us to find personal meaning in our work as leaders and they influence our strategy for success, helping us to define and achieve our goals.

Within your organization, there might be other impactful questions that you want to prioritize as a leader that can help you to filter your decision making through your values and purpose, or organizational vision. Identifying these key questions can help you to ensure that you and your teams stay on track and purposeful in your work. For example, within our organization (Changing Minds Child and Family Services, CMCAFS), we use the following questions to ensure we are making purposeful decisions that fit with our values and vision:

- Are we working with people, teams and organizations who share similar values?

- Is the work meaningful, psychologically responsive and high quality? Are we proud of it? (See the Introduction for a reminder of the definition of 'psychologically responsive'.)

- Is it sustainable (for us), and will it leave a sustainable impact on the organizations we are supporting?

- Are we the best placed to do this work, or could it be better undertaken by another organization or service?

When we are feeling pulled, or in crisis, or where there are differing strong opinions within the team, these questions help to anchor us in our leadership and ensure that we are aligned and purposeful moving forward.

What is a vision?

A team or organizational vision is a mental image of what the team wants to achieve in the near future. Having this future-focused, inspired concept of the organization helps it to develop, grow, adapt and reimagine itself in the context of the changing landscape of its work. The vision may involve both shorter- and longer-term planning. It is one of the key elements in a highly effective strategic plan, and is essentially the desired destination of the organization that shapes the strategy that is the map of how to 'get there'.

When we, as leaders, have a clear vision for the organization, it can help us to make decisions regarding actions and opportunities based on whether they fit or detract from our longer-term goals. It helps us stay on track and keeps our eyes on our desired destination. Having a clear and concise vision helps us to communicate, both within the organization and to others outside, including potential investors or collaborators, what we are trying to achieve. It can guide us through difficult times and even times of crisis when stress is high, providing an 'anchor' to help us to stay on track, and some containment to the team. The vision can also influence the culture of the organization as it can help colleagues to feel more connected and purposeful together, as they can see what they are all working together towards.

Here are some examples of corporate vision statements:

BBC: 'To be the most creative organization in the world.'

Google: 'To provide access to the world's information in one click.'

IKEA: 'To create a better everyday life for the many people.'

Instagram: 'Capture and share the world's moments.'

LinkedIn: 'Create economic opportunity for every member of the global workforce.'

Microsoft: 'To help people throughout the world realize their full potential.'

Nike: 'To bring inspiration and innovation to every athlete in the world.'

Oxfam: 'A just world without poverty.'

Tesla: 'To accelerate the world's transition to sustainable energy.'

Ben & Jerry's: 'Making the best ice cream in the nicest possible way.'

Ford: 'People working together as a lean, global enterprise to make people's lives better through automotive and mobility leadership.'

IBM: 'To be the world's most successful and important information technology company. Successful in helping our customers apply technology to solve their problems. Successful in introducing this extraordinary technology to new customers. Important because we will continue to be the basic resource of much of what is invested in this industry.'

TEAM TASK: DEVELOPING THE TEAM/ORGANIZATION'S VISION

With key people within senior leadership or the whole team, ask your colleagues to think about the following questions, make notes and discuss:

- What do you want the future to look like for your team/organization? (Focus on what it would look like rather than how to get there.)

- Look forward 2–3 years or even 5–10 years. What do you want to achieve?

- How would you want someone to describe your organization in a few years' time?

Writing a vision statement

Once you have discussed this between the colleagues who took part (preferably the whole team, if possible), it is helpful to pull out the themes of the vision ideas to help you to arrive at a clear, concise and aspirational vision statement.

The importance of the context and future thinking

You have probably heard the words 'agile' and 'flexible' a lot in terms of leadership, particularly over the past few years, with the multiple challenges that we have faced as a society (such as the pandemic, cost of living crisis, climate crisis and the growing impact of technology). With the volatile, uncertain, complex and ambiguous (also referred to as VUCA) world that we live in, it is important that we, as leaders, remain aware of what is happening within our sector, adjoining sectors and society as a whole when future planning for our teams and organizations. If organizations are living beings which are influenced by and have an impact on humans (see Chapter 4), it is important for you, as a leader, to consider the psychological impact of both macro- and microcultural pressures and change on the functioning and wellbeing of the organization, the team and the individuals within it. This systemic perspective, considering what is happening and being experienced at every level of the system, is an important part of being psychologically responsive, helping us to consider and navigate complexity in order to achieve greater success.

For example, at the time of writing this chapter (2024), many councils in England have warned that they are facing bankruptcy within the next couple of years. With council budgets already tight, and following many cuts to council services over the past few years, this is likely to have a further catastrophic impact on the social care sector, with associated knock-on effects within health and education. In addition, the ever-increasing use of more complex technology is likely to have a prominent impact on most workplaces within the next few years.

It is crucial to bring your team together to help you to think about how you can recognize, monitor and be aware of potential challenges, threats and opportunities that your organization may encounter. This can help you to identify any potential blind spots or incorrect assumptions, and ensure that you have a much wider understanding of potential issues from a range of perspectives. This is one of the many places where diversity of thinking can really help, where you can talk to people with different backgrounds, life experience, work experience, knowledge and expertise. Before working on a mission statement and further strategy, taking the time to map out the wider landscape in your world of work can help you, as a leader, to be more informed and make better decisions. Involving key stakeholders in this process, particularly those who can bring different perspectives, experiences and ideas – considering those within your wider network who could bring a different view or challenge your thinking – can also be a good idea.

There are many different exercises that you can do as a leader to start to think about this in a more strategic way, such as doing a PESTLE analysis. PESTLE is a strategic decision-making and scenario planning tool, which is used to analyse the environmental factors that could have a significant impact on an organization. The acronym stands for Political, Economic, Sociological, Technological, Legal and

Environmental. Using a PESTLE template[1] can help you to think through each area with your team (or other stakeholders) in turn, to use their knowledge, expertise and perspectives to create a greater understanding of the wider context and likely future challenges or opportunities for your organization.

We would recommend that, as a minimum, doing a SWOT analysis with a few key individuals would give you some good data that you can then hold in mind when considering the direction you want your organization to go in the future, and how to get there.

TEAM TASK: SWOT ANALYSIS

Strengths: What particular strengths or resources does the team/organization have? What makes you resilient? What are your unique selling points?

Weaknesses: What are the potential areas of weakness within the team/organization? What could be the potential pitfalls?

Opportunities: Considering the current and likely future climate, what opportunities could be available for the team/organization? What opportunities could you take advantage of?

Threats: What potential threats might be on the horizon for the team/organization? What do you need to be aware of/continue to monitor? Consider some likely scenarios that could play out that could cause some challenge for your team/organization.

The OST of VMOST: Moving to action

Although we are not going to cover it in depth here (that would be another full book!), when we, as leaders, have a clear vision and mission, the next step is to use this to consider what our strategy needs to be (i.e., how we get there). A common acronym used when thinking

---

1   For information and a template for a PESTLE analysis, see: www.cipd.org/uk/knowledge/factsheets/pestle-analysis-factsheet

about strategic planning is VMOST, which stands for Vision, Mission, Objectives, Strategies and Tactics. Working your way through this process ensures that your strategy is well aligned with your overall vision and mission, making it more purposeful and ensuring that you stay on track. It helps you to identify key objectives that you are working towards and consider how to measure against these to assess whether you are making progress in the right direction. It also identifies clear areas to focus on, and tactics (smaller actions) that can be allocated to individuals with timescales.

When strategizing, it can be helpful to recognize the context that we are working within in this ever-changing world. We cannot fully guarantee what the future will look like for our service or team, however much scoping or planning we do. Nor can we promise that our initial strategic plans will lead to the desired outcome, as there are too many variables that might affect it. For example, most of us could not have predicted that Covid-19 would occur at that time, affecting our lives and work in the diverse ways that it did. Therefore, it is essential to be mindful of the ever-changing context that we are in, and to continue to consult with others, seek feedback, look at outcomes and regularly review our strategy and plans going forward to ensure that they are still relevant, considering the current context and likely future.

Summary

In recent decades, organizational psychology has recognized that leaders investing time and energy in developing their organizational/team mission, vision and values can help them to build connection and greater cohesion between people who are working together. Our team can develop a shared sense of purpose and a plan to achieve their goals, which considers a wide range of factors within the culture of their work. Having such a clear shared purpose, goal and plan meets our need for connection and personal meaning in our work, and therefore helps team members to feel more confident, to achieve their goals and experience success. When, as both leaders and team members, we feel connected, confident and purposeful, and we have a considered strategy, we are more able to be agile and adaptable when we are faced with new information or challenges. This enables us to be more resilient and therefore increases our opportunities for success. Clinical psychology theory and practice echo the positive impact of connection, purpose and values on our individual well-being, self-worth and agency. We have drawn on acceptance and commitment therapy (ACT), typically applied to support individual psychological wellbeing, to demonstrate how this knowledge can also be applied at a team or organizational level. Therefore, developing clarity as a leader regarding your and your team's mission, vision and values not only supports a team's likelihood of success, but also develops their resilience and psychological wellbeing.

In the next chapter, we consider relationship dynamics within teams/organizations, and look more closely at the factors that help us to develop individual and team resilience from a psychological perspective.

References and recommended reading

Collins, J. (2024) 'The Hedgehog Concept.' www.jimcollins.com/concepts/the-hedgehog-concept.html

Dearlove, D. (2023) *Certain Uncertainty: Leading with Agility and Resilience in an Unpredictable World*. Hoboken, NJ: John Wiley & Sons.

Hayes, S. C. and Strosahl, K. D. (eds) (2004) *A Practical Guide to Acceptance and Commitment Therapy*. New York: Springer Science + Business Media, Inc.

Sinek, S. (2011) *Start With Why: How Greater Leaders Inspire Everyone to Take Action*. New York: Penguin Books.

CHAPTER 4

Observing Relational Dynamics

In the previous chapter, we articulated the importance of the relationships and connection within a team and how you, as leaders, can enable this through developing a shared purpose, values and plan. In this chapter, we take a closer look at how the psychological understanding of relationships between individuals and within teams, organizations and wider systems can support your work as a leader. We draw on psychological therapeutic models regarding relational dynamics, helping to understand these dynamics, recognize them and resist being pulled into unhelpful dynamics, and to be proactive as a leader in addressing them when they do arise. The chapter covers the key components of individual and team resilience, and considers how we can build team and organizational resilience to buffer against future challenges.

The importance of team relationships

The 2022 Microsoft Work Trend Index Annual Report demonstrated significant benefits of thriving relationships within teams and organizations. The respondents were asked questions such as 'Would you say you are thriving or struggling with the following types of bonds or relationships at work?', and were then subsequently grouped into either the 'Thriving relationships at work' or the 'Struggling relationships at work' group. The respondents were then asked how much they agreed or disagreed with statements about positive wellbeing, productivity and their likelihood of staying with the organization over the next year. The employees who perceived themselves to have good relationships had significantly more positive responses to the questions asked. They reported being currently more fulfilled by work than before the Covid-19 pandemic, more satisfied with their employer and more optimistic that work stress would improve over the next year.

An emphasis on team and organizational relationships bears fruit. It is often difficult to feel that there is time for creating both formal and informal opportunities to connect with our colleagues, but the evidence from research is that not only do better relationships impact positively on wellbeing and morale within a team, but they also bolster employees' perceptions of resilience, optimism, belonging, productivity and commitment to the organization. So, can we really afford not to prioritize time for building and nurturing relationships in our teams?

Relational dynamics

When two or more people have a relationship with one another there are patterns of behaviour between them that influence and impact how they interact, communicate and relate. These are known as 'relational dynamics'. We can see these dynamics between a parent and child, between children, adults, partners, friends and, of course, between teams and organizations and wider systems. The patterns of these relationships have a significant effect on what it feels like to be part of the relationship, team or organization, but also on the performance and productivity of the team. Therefore, paying attention to how human beings interact with one another, and what helps human beings to feel good and perform well, is key to leadership.

When thinking about our own practice and supporting other teams and organizations, we have found it helpful to think about some of the models of intra- (between individuals) and interpersonal (internal to the individual) dynamics that we often refer to in our work as clinical psychologists. These models help us understand the internal dynamics that can be experienced by an individual, but are just as relevant to understanding the dynamics that can play out between individuals, in families, within teams and within or between organizations too. In fact, we often think of intrapersonal dynamics as being an internalized version of the interpersonal dynamics we have experienced in our formative personal and work relationships.

As we have stated previously within this book, we are interested in a systemic perspective, and how as leaders we should always think about how the events in one part of the system impact the other parts of the system, from the individual to the wider culture. We recognize that the events within an organization will impact and change the behaviour and experiences of team members, and that this will also have a knock-on effect for the individual clients of the team. It is this understanding of how dynamics ripple between individuals and groups, and the knowledge that we effect change most successfully when we make interventions at every level of the system, which is the basis for a systemic perspective.

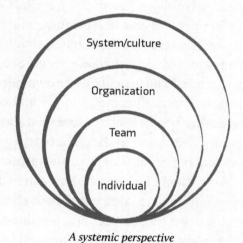

A systemic perspective

All behaviour is understandable with context

Our behaviour and how we interact with others is shaped so much by our previous experience – our early childhood experiences both within our families and outside of the family – but also in our adult relationships and work experiences. What we know is that although sometimes the behaviour of individuals in our team, of the team as a whole, or even of ourselves, may seem strange or frustrating, there will be a context behind it. There will be something that has happened (either historically, more recently, or both) that will have shaped the behaviour that we see. Therefore, if we can allow ourselves to acknowledge that 'all behaviour is understandable with context', it can bring us to a more empathic position. We might not fully know the context, or what has happened to bring about this behaviour, but we can empathize that something must have happened that has led the person to act in this way. This does not mean that the behaviour is excused or ignored, but this perspective helps us to give the best possible interpretation of someone's actions, and doing so helps us to discuss and challenge with connection rather than disconnection.

UNDERSTANDING BEHAVIOUR IN CONTEXT

For example, our colleague Janet[1] may have had early experiences with her parents and sick brother, which are likely unknown to her manager and colleagues, that have shaped her into feeling ignored and not good enough. She might find it hard to understand and articulate her own needs, but she feels threatened by other people's success and confidence, and how easy other people seem to find relationships. Janet finds relationships hard, and so she tends to try to find people (both in work and her life outside) that she respects, and tries her best to make them like her too. This can include doing things like gossiping and making jokes about other staff with them and trying to get them on her side. She doesn't feel good enough and can therefore feel easily shamed by situations and other people, causing her to withdraw or covertly 'throw other people under the bus', blaming them or trying to make them look bad. As her leader, I may not know the cause of her lack of confidence and self-worth, but I can see the evidence of it in her behaviour and communication within work.

---

[1] A made-up name, for purposes of anonymity.

Understanding that people who are being pulled into pleasing others all the time and not holding their boundaries or own needs as important too, or (the other end of the continuum) people withdrawing, disconnecting or using bravado to cover their human vulnerability, may indicate a lack of confidence and self-worth, which helps us as leaders to understand how we might support their development (see the section 'The Boundary Seesaw' later in this chapter for more detail).

As Janet's manager, I can apply the knowledge that it is likely that a lack of self-worth and confidence is behind her 'people-pleasing' behaviour to plan how I can support her development. I might consider how I take steps, so I do not inadvertently reinforce her people-pleasing behaviour. I might raise with her in our supervision that I have noticed she may sometimes feel the need to give others what they want, even when it might not fit with her needs. I might use a specific example of when she agreed to help someone with their work despite not having enough time to complete her own work. I would reflect with her how her willingness to help others may sometimes come at an unequal cost to her, and explore her perspective. I might think with her about ways in which to manage these scenarios, perhaps using some coaching skills (see Chapter 1) to help her to generate some of her own potential solutions. For example, this could be for her to explain to other team members that while she would like to help them, unfortunately she is under pressure and at risk of not meeting her own deadline. We might come back to this in future supervision sessions to think about how she has experimented with this and how she feels about it now. I might acknowledge and praise her when she has managed to resist pleasing others at too great a cost to herself. I can also seek to reinforce her confidence and self-worth in my supervision sessions, giving her honest and positive feedback about her work and acknowledging achievements. This increased self-worth will hopefully help Janet to feel less need to overstep her own boundaries and needs in service of other people.

In clinical psychology we often engage in psychological formulation to help us to understand the source of behaviours and feelings, how people have made sense of their experiences, and what reinforces these behaviours or dynamics. As leaders we are unlikely to know the background to the behaviours and dynamics we observe in our staff, and we do not need to know. That is not our business unless someone feels it is important information to give to bring context and understanding. We would not encourage leaders to ask personal questions about their team member's childhood and where relationship patterns have come from. It is sufficient to tentatively acknowledge the observable patterns in relationship dynamics with curiosity and empathy. If we understand that certain patterns of behaviour, in general terms, may often signify a lack of confidence, feeling unsafe or not feeling good enough, we can carefully wonder with our staff member about how we might be able to help them to feel more confident and what steps they might take within work to build a more positive sense of themselves. For example, it may be more obvious that individuals who seek constant checking in and reassurance may lack confidence in themselves and their work; however, a lack of confidence can also be expressed through behaviours intended to keep the person 'safer'. This may look like a team member who is less connected to the team and keeps themselves separate, motivated by keeping others at bay in order not to be vulnerable to their judgement. Bravado and 'unchecked confidence' can also be an indication of a lack of self-worth. When we do not feel good enough and confident in ourselves to be physically or psychologically safe with others, we can sometimes adopt a mask of fake confidence and toughness (physical or psychological) in order to help us to feel safe.

All these examples are actually expressions of a lack of self-worth and confidence despite them appearing very different on the surface. When individuals are often repeating any of these behaviours, they require feedback from their managers and those around them that helps to boost their real sense of confidence, worth and ability, despite the behaviour and relationship patterns we notice (and tentatively acknowledge with them, in our supervision or appraisals, with curiosity and empathy) being quite different from one another.

We can also recognize that our colleague may need more positive feedback and opportunities to experience achievement and success (see Chapter 1) and help them to experience such opportunities within work, directly from us and from other colleagues. We may also consider with them how to support them to build more trusting relationships with others in the team. Both approaches, verbal reflection and direct action, can help an individual to develop and perform better within the team, without the leader knowing the backstory of the interpersonal behaviours and dynamics that person brings.

While understanding the roots of difficulties can be helpful at times, it is not always possible or appropriate to go investigating this information. It is often enough to be aware of the difficulty in front of us and seek to build forward from the point we are at. Using our knowledge of people to understand the most likely human emotion at play, we must build foundations of positive self-worth and agency through positive feedback, experiences and skills development.

The Boundary Seesaw

We have found the concept of the Boundary Seesaw very helpful to recognize and name unhelpful 'pulls' in relationships (Hamilton 2010). These are common pulls that we can see played out in all kinds of relationships – personal, professional and societal – but when we are in caring roles, we may be especially prone to these dynamics, and therefore to be aware of them and able to discuss them is even more important. The concept of the Boundary Seesaw has helped us to recognize in ourselves as leaders and within the teams we are supporting that we may be being pulled into an unhelpful position that does not best serve us or the person we are supporting despite best intentions. It helps us to recognize what may be going wrong and gives us a framework to explore this more thoroughly. Not only does it help us to understand what we need to resist, but it also helps us to consider a more helpful position and explore what questions, concerns and perspectives that balanced position might raise for us.

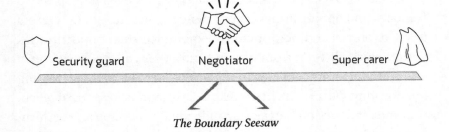

Security guard   Negotiator   Super carer

The Boundary Seesaw

The super carer

At either end of the seesaw, we are being pulled away from centring the client/patient/child and we may inadvertently become 'caught up' in serving our own needs to protect ourselves. At the 'super carer' end of the seesaw we become enmeshed with the needs and perspective of the individual or group. We might over-identify with them, become highly protective and defensive of them, see ourselves as having a 'special relationship' with them and being their 'saviour'. When we are pulled towards this polarized position, we overstep boundaries, work outside of work hours, have contact with clients in personal time or via personal messages, or perhaps diminish the work of our co-workers. We can inadvertently be serving our own needs to be 'the good guy' and even be rather self-righteous. This 'super carer' position also undermines the agency and autonomy of the individual we are looking to support. We are not scaffolding the individual to enable their confidence to articulate their needs and wishes, decision making, responsibility taking and boundary setting, but instead playing the hero and doing it all for them, or at least too much. This is not serving our clients well even though they may wish to be 'rescued'.

Our intentions might be to meet the needs of our client/patient/child, but we can, in fact, be serving our own needs by using our personal coping styles such as being the 'good guy' and being a saviour. We should also be aware that when the caring relationship is serving our own needs rather than supporting the client's development and overall wellbeing, we are often transgressing boundaries and failing to enable our client's agency. This dynamic can inadvertently mirror the dynamics of harm and abusive relationships, when our client's wellbeing was subverted in service of someone else's dominant needs.

Many of the individuals we are supporting in health, education and social care may have experienced unhealthy relationship dynamics and be trying to recover from them. Therefore, if we inadvertently repeat unhealthy dynamics, even if to a much lesser extent, not only are we failing to support the agency and development of the individual, but we are also reinforcing an already learned dysfunctional interpersonal dynamic for them. Ultimately this over-identification with the client and transgressing of boundaries cannot be maintained and we become overwhelmed and 'burnt out', at which point we are likely to swing to the other end of the Boundary Seesaw, to the disconnected 'security guard' position, in an attempt to protect ourselves.

The security guard
'Disconnection' characterizes the 'security guard' end of the Boundary Seesaw. Instead of becoming enmeshed with the client as the 'super carer' does, we lose our ability to connect and empathize with the individual we are looking to support. At this end of the seesaw we become focused on rigid rules, holding on to control and tightening boundaries. We might become more formal, cut-off and cold, focusing on the need for tight practices, rules and control in order to help the client or team. At this end of the Boundary Seesaw we are emotionally distancing ourselves from the people we are meant to be serving. We might do this by being uncaring, but also by making light of or being dismissive of their needs and experiences. We can find ourselves at this end of the seesaw when we are worn out and experiencing 'compassion fatigue', perhaps due to being mentally and emotionally overloaded due to factors and demands both in and outside work.

The negotiator
The 'negotiator' position attempts to synthesize the positive aspects of both the care of one end of the seesaw and the boundaries of the other. If you can be in this position, then you are willing to recognize the need for both, and the nuance and negotiation required to hold this balanced position. Professional relationships are neither too close, nor too distant, and professional judgement is applied,

resulting in a sense of safety, predictability and empowerment for the client, staff member or participant, reducing the risk of harm. The negotiator can be agile and adapt according to the context, and also consider the needs of the individual, moving along the seesaw in a conscious way, depending on what is required by the given situation, without being pulled to the extremes of the seesaw. The negotiator is mindful of when they or others may be getting pulled to one end or the other and is able to reflect by themselves and discuss with others what might be happening in the context for this to occur. This allows the negotiator to rebalance themselves at the relevant point on the seesaw from which they can consider all logical and emotional information.

As a leader, we may also feel these pulls to either side of the seesaw. We can apply this reflective model when thinking about both our relationship with the clients we are trying to serve, and also with our teams and colleagues. Sometimes we may feel pulled into a rescuing role with our team, where we might overstep boundaries and over-care or take over and do things for them (which has the potential to be disempowering and can lead to feelings of unsafety or emotional exhaustion for the leader). At other times, we may feel frustrated and overwhelmed and might be pulled to a more disconnected, cut-off place to protect ourselves.

It is important to acknowledge that human beings will always be pulled towards the ends of the continuum at times, no matter how experienced and aware we are. This is an inevitable result of human dynamics and is not evidence of poor work. However, if we stay too near the ends of the seesaw without recognizing and adjusting our position, this can cause problems. It is incumbent on us to recognize the impact of this on others, and to face the fact that we may be unconsciously serving our own needs, to be the 'super carer' rescuer or to be in control and disconnected, like the 'security guard'. We might get pulled into patterns of behaviours in relationships that have their roots in our earlier experiences, how we see ourselves, or how we have learned to cope with stress. This is where self-reflection as a leader is extremely important to recognize and resist unhealthy dynamics that do not serve the staff or clients we are supporting. Being able to share this and similar models within our teams can help us to be able to name, reflect and think through our positions within these dynamics together, and hold each other to account when we might be pulled in unhelpful ways. Developing self-reflection skills as an individual, within supervision and as a team, is an important part of being a psychologically responsive leader.

Headteacher Maxine O'Neill gave us an example of how she observed staff being pulled to one end or other of the Boundary Seesaw, but also how she has used such concepts to help her to understand what is going on and what needs to change for the dynamic to improve for both the student and teacher.

Maxine O'Neill, Headteacher, Hope School, Liverpool, UK: Use of relational models

I had an intelligent member of staff who was boundaries- and rules-oriented, but this meant she could be a little rigid at times, towards the 'security guard' end of the seesaw. She had a child in her class who came from an inner-city area, and his social context meant he presented as tough and there were concerns that he was at risk of becoming involved in crime in the future. The teacher's 'prison guard' approach made the child go into a 'tough guy' role, and every rule she put in place to try to contain him, he would meet with an attitude of 'I'm tough and I don't need this, and I don't need that.' The teacher was very reflective and talked with me about the dynamic between them. As a result, she tried to move away from the 'prison guard' position and let him have a bit more playfulness, a bit more freedom, and also focused on building up a relationship with his mum, which has been really difficult because his mum doesn't trust many people. This shift in the teacher's behaviour led to the boy softening and being a little more relaxed. This led to him going into an upset emotional response rather than a 'fight' emotional response when he found things difficult. The teacher initially responded to this by moving to the 'super carer' end of the seesaw, where she would sit, and she would rock him, and she would soothe him. But then she'd come to me and say she didn't think it was fair to put in boundaries for him because emotionally he was so young, and he could not manage things. The boy was also using lots of language around self-injury and self-harm. The teacher was worried about him; she was feeling very emotional herself and burnt out, and also worried that if she went back to being rules-focused he would just mask his emotional distress with bravado again.

The teacher and I had a really good conversation about the need to be more in the 'negotiator' position, and have both boundaries and playfulness with him and the class, and as a result things shifted in a positive direction. The child had previously struggled to build emotional relationships, but then he started to make real friendships within the class because he had the opportunity to be playful as well as being contained and containing himself more. He took more control and responsibility while also enjoying the relationship with his teacher, leaning into some nurture when needed. Previously, when the teacher moved into 'super carer', the boy stayed in a more baby-like state and didn't make relationships with his peers, as he was then very emotional all the time and seeking out relationships with adults to soothe him. But when his teacher and he were relating at the 'prison guard' end of the seesaw, he couldn't make relationships because everything was defensive and hard.

The teacher being able to take a more balanced 'negotiator' position helped him to take that more balanced position too. He was not so defensive and could accept some boundaries, but he could also seek regulation when needed and self-regulate more of the time – and as a result he developed peer relationships that were lovely and playful. This took time over a period of months. But, led by her interaction, the boy mirrored his teacher's position. The teacher was also very reflective and learned a lot. She learned to recognize more easily when she was naturally pulling to the more rigid and rule-based end of the spectrum with her class, and that she had to bring in more playfulness and fun to get back to a better balance.

I think you can see this same dynamic often play out between schools and parents, for example in parent–teacher forums. Parents might come in with a complaint that the school responds defensively to, or schools start off being defensive when parents raise an issue, and we end up having a relationship at the more disconnected end of the Boundary Seesaw – teachers feeling 'How dare you challenge me' and parents feeling dictated to, criticized or unheard. Things then escalate very quickly. How the school sets that stall and that relationship to begin with creates this whole dynamic. We set a culture for how parents can raise an issue or how they can reach out.

The Karpman Drama Triangle

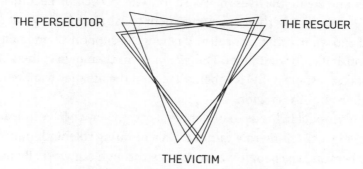

THE PERSECUTOR   THE RESCUER

THE VICTIM

The Karpman Drama Triangle

There are many parallels between psychological therapeutic models that help us to understand both internal and external relational dynamics. Many dynamic therapeutic models would hypothesize that we internalize our primary relationships into internal relationships with ourselves. The Karpman Drama Triangle (Karpman 1968), which was developed from transactional analysis, recognizes the unconscious roles and positions we might adopt within relationships similar to the Boundary Seesaw. The Drama Triangle articulates well how the position we take up in our leadership role can 'project' others into certain roles too, thereby highlighting the impact of our actions on others.

The *'rescuer'* position is defined by needing to 'save' people perceived as vulnerable. The *'rescuer'* works hard and offers unneeded/

unrequested 'help', often doing for or doing to others rather than scaffolding other people's agency. The *'persecutor'* uses their power to judge and criticise others, often without understanding of why the actions occurred or assuming negative intentions of the other individual. The *'victim'* is overwhelmed by their own vulnerability and does not take responsibility for their own situation or agency to change it.

The way out of these roles is to stay away from the extreme positions and move towards the middle. The *'rescuer'* then uses their care and concern to take on the role of *coach*. The *coach*, instead of trying to rescue others, sees others as empowered creators in charge of their own lives, and seeks to support them to take responsibility for themselves and create the lives they wish for. The *'persecutor'* becomes the *challenger* and uses their encouragement to ask the *'victim'* what they need and want, bringing healthy challenge to support them in taking responsibility for their lives. The *'victim'* owns their own vulnerability and takes responsibility for themselves and the life they want to lead, and becomes the *creator*.

This model helps us to understand the power we have as leaders in taking a coaching role rather than a rescuing role with our team members and the people we are serving through our work. By resisting the pull to rescue, we help to create agency within the individual. To have true agency we are also required to acknowledge our own responsibility. If we blame others, project responsibility onto them and see ourselves only as the victim of other people's actions, we are unable to fully embrace our own agency.

Some professionals have told us they prefer to use either the Boundary Seesaw or the Drama Triangle with their colleagues to discuss relationship dynamics, so we thought it important to include both models, despite the overlap.

Understanding these interpersonal dynamics and how these models can play out within our work with our clients or within our working relationships allows us to notice them more often when they are occurring. Once we are more aware of these dynamics starting to play out, we are able to adjust our position, change our behaviour and resist the pull. It may also be helpful to name what is going on in relationships with others: 'I may be being pulled here into rescuing and I need to be aware of that' or 'I wonder if we, as a team, are being pulled into being a bit rigid as we are worried other professionals are being pulled to the rescuer role.' Sometimes just recognizing and resisting these pulls, discussing them in supervision or naming them with colleagues can really help change dynamics and help us to take a more helpful and conscious approach to our relationships in our leadership roles.

Parallel processes

Within psychology, we recognize that in a relationship, one person, often unconsciously, recreates or parallels the difficulties and feelings of the other. In a supervision setting, the supervisee's transference may be thought and felt by the supervisor, and the supervisor's countertransference may be experienced by the supervisee. This is the parallel process. This is also true on a group basis, whereby the experiences, thoughts and feelings of the client group are often reflected in the thoughts and feelings of the staff group. It is important for leaders to be aware of this parallel process with clients when working in education, health and social care, but also to recognise that this parallel process can occur between different levels of an organization, such as with staff and managers.

We have found the work of Dr Sandra Bloom (who kindly wrote the Foreword for this book) extremely valuable in understanding that these relationship dynamics play out not just between individuals, but also between teams and organizations. Dr Bloom emphasizes the importance of seeing teams and organizations as *living things* that can be affected by stress just as we as individuals can be impacted. Within her work, she communicates that 'Chronic stress stealthily robs an organization of basic interpersonal safety and trust and thereby robs an organization of health. Organizations, like individuals, can be traumatized, and the result of traumatic experience can be as devastating for organizations as it is for individuals' (2011, p.105).

Emotions, stress and trauma are contagious, and this is the basis for transference and countertransference, and therefore the parallel process. This is usually quite an unconscious process, but our bodies and brains are sensitive, and react, to the bodies and brains we connect with. Therefore, when I walk into a room and my two colleagues are feeling stressed out and anxious, soon I am likely to start to develop similar feelings, thoughts and behaviours. I might notice my body starting to feel tense, my thoughts becoming more threat-based, and I might start to behave in an anxious way (such as pacing or wanting to leave). When we are working with highly stressed and traumatized groups of people, we, too, are likely to experience stress reactions, as discussed in the Boundary Seesaw, where we might either become too enmeshed or too disconnected. These are both reactions to 'threat' and a heightened threat system (fight, flight, freeze or flop). It is not surprising, therefore, that teams and organizations that work with individuals or groups that have a heightened threat response, for whatever reason, will feel and show a reaction to this sense of threat. Additionally, Dr Bloom also acknowledges that such organizations are often under their own stress/threat. They may be experiencing stressors such as significant cuts, large waiting lists, financial pressures, staffing issues or the aftermath of an incident. The organization's stress will be 'held' by the senior leadership team and has the potential to 'ripple' down the organization, as staff feel the pressures, stress and emotions felt by the senior leadership team too.

For example, if around exam time, pupils were feeling stressed, anxious, overly emotional and overwhelmed, fragmented, experiencing feelings of not being good enough etc., then it is likely that this will be felt within the staff team too. Similarly, if a school is going through a particularly difficult period, with lots of uncertainty about jobs and a change in management, the school as a whole may feel unsafe, stuck, crisis-driven and fragmented. Staff may feel overwhelmed, unsafe and defensive, and may begin working in silos, feeling directionless or reactive. These feelings and behaviours may 'ripple' down and be felt at all levels of the school, leading to the pupils feeling unsafe, anxious and overwhelmed without the usual containment and safety being provided by their teachers. It is therefore important to acknowledge this, be aware of what is happening, and consider how we support all levels of a system.

Dr Bloom (2013a) identifies the seven key domains of how this 'ripple effect' or parallel process may present within individuals and within a stressed or traumatized organizational context:

1. *Lack of safety and trust and being crisis-driven.* Feeling unsafe and struggling to trust in others is an extremely common reaction to threat, whether it be trauma or stress. Our innate threat response (fight, flight, freeze or flop) is activated, and we feel like we are walking on unsteady ground. We cannot trust in others, the world and sometimes ourselves to keep us safe, and so we can become sensitized to threat and very reactive in our responses to people and events without taking time to think things through and act proactively. We can lurch from one issue to the next. We, our team and our organization are in survival mode.

2. *Loss of emotional management.* We struggle to manage our overwhelming emotions, to soothe/regulate ourselves, to benefit from co-regulation from others or to draw on our emotional intelligence. This is because we are in survival mode, and so those higher-level brain functions in the cerebral cortex are offline to us, or at least much harder to access. This heightened emotional state and lack of regulation inevitably negatively impacts our relationships and our ability to problem solve, which impacts our cognitive functioning.

3. *Problems with cognition, dissociation and amnesia.* We lose sight of the bigger picture and an ability to think things through. Instead, we came become 'blinkered' or dissociate from part of the information, particularly if the information is unwanted, difficult or challenging. We fail to notice, think and learn, and instead behave reactively, repeating unhelpful patterns over and over, demonstrating a lack of learning. When we fail to recognize all the available information and reality of the

situation, it becomes almost impossible to name and discuss it with our colleagues and team members.

4. *Individual and group miscommunication and conflict.* When we are feeling under, and behaving from a place of, threat, our ability to communicate, how we communicate and what we communicate (both verbally and non-verbally) are affected. This means that open, clear communication becomes much more difficult, which can lead to people feeling 'in the dark', experiencing a lack of purpose, feeling unvalued or even undermined. When communication is unclear or poor, a team's ability to recognize and talk about the very issues causing them problems reduces or fails completely.

5. *Authoritarianism, learned helplessness and silent dissent.* These conditions of threat and trauma lead many of us to fall into patterns of control or passivity. Some of us might often/sometimes become controlling in our behaviour and relationships to deal with the stress of the situation, while other people may take on a more passive role. The latter may feel they have no agency to change the situation so there is little point in trying. This can present as either passive behaviour, helpless and inert, or it can present as 'passive aggression', as the individual in the use of subtle control to influence behaviour, while presenting a compliant and agreeable front. An example of this is 'silent quitting', where the team member may continue to be present and put in minimum effort, but they don't actively participate in the team, discussion, meetings and activities.

6. *Punishment, revenge and organizational injustice.* When the threat is high and we feel fear and pressure, we can react with anger to blame, punish and seek to displace our negative feelings on to others. We can seek to blame others without looking at our own or joint responsibility. This can be done overtly or more covertly, of course. We can sabotage other people or the work we are doing, and this can be conscious or often unconscious as a defensive reaction to the overwhelming emotions we are feeling in the situation. Teams and organizations can

become ethically compromised because they are not holding the bigger picture and taking responsibility but looking to apportion blame and project responsibility on to other team members, teams, organizations and even clients.

7. *Unresolved grief, re-enactment and decline.* We may end up feeling stuck in this traumatic situation with feelings of loss and grief, unable to learn and move forward. We become dissatisfied with our work and have feelings of failure, repeating ineffective patterns and strategies. Ultimately this leads to burnout.

There are many ways we might react to a high level of stress and trauma, and by understanding these typical expressions of stress and the manner in which they may impact our functioning, we are more likely to recognize the dynamics at play. For example, when there are changes in team membership, with some colleagues leaving and new ones joining, a team can feel less safe and more stressed. We might see our colleagues feeling less emotionally regulated and more mistrustful of the team, the leadership or the new staff members. This can lead to individuals undermining the leadership by challenging either directly, or more covertly by voicing their disquiet to others or disengaging to some extent from the tasks required by the leader. Our colleagues may be more reactive and defensive in their behaviour, leading to more challenging communication within the team. Our colleagues may struggle to feel a strong sense of purpose or hold a wider picture of the team and their work due to feeling unsettled by the changes.

Sharing this model within your team can make it easier to be able to talk through this together in a normalizing, non-judgemental way, and then think together about how to 'catch' these patterns as they are starting to occur and choose to do something differently:

We work in a sector that can be really stressful at times, and our work is likely to have an impact on us. When teams and organizations are under stress, they are affected by this, too, and these are some of the common ways in which this can play out. It is likely that we, too, may fall into some of these patterns at times, as we are all vulnerable to stress. Which do you think it is more likely that we may fall into? Or which have you seen us fall into before?

As leaders, if we can recognize, name and normalize these patterns, this allows us to 'work through' them, take action to reduce the impact, 'create buffers' and try to be less pulled into unhelpful dynamics, being less reactive, and more thoughtful and proactive. We often talk about how working in organizations supporting young people and families (and adults) who have experienced stress and trauma is difficult, and it is likely to have an impact on us and our teams. These patterns will be likely to play out at times, as they are how humans behave when under threat. It is going to get messy, and all we can do is acknowledge the messiness, try to understand the patterns that our teams and ourselves are likely to fall into, put proactive strategies in place, and try to be less messy than the rest. When organizations deny the impact of stress and trauma, this usually means that it is hidden or that they are in denial (see the section "A false sense of safety" in Chapter 9).

SELF-REFLECTION

- Looking through Dr Sandra Bloom's seven key domains, which resonate with you? Which have you seen play out within the teams in which you have worked before?

- Which have you seen play out in your current team? Or which do you think would be more likely to occur if your team was feeling under threat or stress?

- What might you want to be mindful of? Or for your team to be mindful of?

- What proactive strategies could you put in place to address some of these areas? (Don't worry, we will consider lots of strategies within the book too.)

A developmental sequence in small groups

When, as leaders, we are considering the dynamics at play within our teams, it can also be helpful to understand where the team is in its development and progress. The story of the team and the stage of development it is currently in will shape some of the processes, challenges and emotional and behavioural dynamics at play.

As we will discuss in Chapter 8, the story of a team is important to understand, and helps us to articulate and maintain a sense of purpose, navigate challenges, and even contain and manage tricky relationship dynamics. Psychologist Bruce Tuckman suggested that there are different phases within the life of a team, and came up with the memorable phrase 'forming, storming, norming and performing', which describes the path that teams follow on their way to high performance (2001). Later, he added a fifth stage, 'adjourning' (also known as 'mourning'), to mark the end of a team's journey. Tucker's model frames from the start of the group's coming together to the end of the group's project or work together. The process is not linear, and the group may go back and forth through the stages depending on the team's journey.

During the 'forming' stage, typically the team will focus on the purpose of the team and their work, how the team will be organized, discussing short-term goals, delegating responsibilities and outlining accountability. There may be a discussion defining how the team will organize their time and meetings and the resources they have available to them.

Within the 'storming' stage there are typically some 'push and pull' dynamics, where some of the 'forming' stage outcomes are challenged. This includes some challenge of authority, resisting opinions and suggesting improvements. There may be some arguments and disagreements between team members, some competition between colleagues, and even a negative mindset regarding the team and the team's potential for success. This disagreement can lead to the formation of smaller teams within the team, and some resistance to taking on tasks. External factors and the wider culture of the company can play a significant role in helping the team to navigate this stage.

The 'norming' stage is characterized by team members being more able to offer and accept constructive criticism, and having more open communication as a team and between individuals in the team. We see better working relationships with greater support and trust for one another, as team members attempt to avoid conflict where possible, for the greater good of the team. There is therefore an improved team ethos, cohesion and spirit, and the team can begin to establish and maintain team expectations and rules.

Characteristics of the 'performing' stage are when team members can clearly identify their role within the team and appreciate their own and other team members' strengths and weaknesses. Members now have the ability to prevent, or continue working through, issues that arise, and the team demonstrates greater working relationships and support for each other. The energy within the team is directed towards the attainment of goals, and as such, the members have adopted procedures for making decisions, including how to share leadership responsibilities and work delegation. The individual team members have a sense of freedom and of belonging.

The 'adjourning' (or 'mourning') stage is the final stage of Tuckman's group development model. The team has hopefully completed their project, met their goals, and are ready to celebrate. The team may learn by reflecting on what went well and what they might do differently next time. This ending stage can feel both celebratory and/or be very challenging, especially if the team does not feel they have met the goals they set for themselves. Either way, the ending, disbanding or significant change within a team's form and purpose can be difficult and emotionally unsettling for the team members. Clear structure, containment and reflection are important at this stage of the team's development.

Understanding Tuckman's stages of group development can help teams run more smoothly and helps leaders to understand where the team is currently at, normalizing any challenges and helping leaders to think about how best to support the team to move towards the performing stage.

SELF-REFLECTION

- Where is your team currently in their journey, using Tuckman's stages of development?

- What do you notice in the behaviours and dynamics of the team at this stage?

- What causes your team to move between the stages in either direction?

- If you are in the forming, storming or norming phases, how could you support your team towards performing?

We can influence the team to support its moving towards the 'performing' stage and resist becoming stuck. As the leader, or as part of the senior leadership team, we can review where the team is and how we might support them by ensuring that some of the behaviours and practices listed in the box below are happening. There are various team and individual activities within this book to help you think about how you might want to improve communication within your team, create a shared vision and purpose, encourage a sense of belonging and togetherness within your team and enable team members to take on responsibilities and support the development of a project or skills within the team. Here are some ideas regarding how you might support your team towards their performance goals.

TEAM TASK: FORMING TO PERFORMING

Forming to storming:

- Maintain clear communication.

- Provide opportunities to build relationships and get to know one another (formal and more informal).

121

- Establish clear expectations, objectives, roles and responsibilities.
- Share vision – and how an individual and the team's work will contribute to the bigger picture.
- Get to know individuals and their strengths.

Storming to norming:

- Build trust and psychological safety (see Chapters 7 and 9).
- Ask for support from team members – modelling asking for help/ not always knowing the answer.
- Focus on short-term targets and end goals.
- Have clarity around individual roles and objectives.
- Normalize interpersonal and team dynamics that can play out.
- Provide coaching for individuals.
- Support the team to work through conflict and challenge.
- Provide opportunities for collaboration.
- Make sure all have a voice – try to encourage everyone to speak up and contribute.
- Inspire the team through the 'Why' – connect to the purpose.

Norming to performing:

- Continue to provide opportunities to build relationships and connections within the team (both formal and informal).
- Delegate and encourage others to lead on projects and take on responsibilities.
- Encourage collaboration.
- Ensure that there is clarity around objectives and strategy.
- Use outcomes to drive forward targets – share these with the team, and celebrate achievements and positive feedback.

- Involve your team in strategy discussions and problem solving.

- Set objectives and targets, both for individuals and for the wider team.

When understanding teams and organizations as living beings, as Dr Bloom suggests, it is also helpful to see them as having a life cycle. Understanding the phases of the life cycle and the typical attributes of these phases can help us, as leaders, to better understand the dynamics we are observing and experiencing within a team. In turn, this helps us to determine the best course of action in response to these dynamics. Maybe action is required to move the team along and diminish the difficulty of the challenging dynamic. Other times the leader (or team) may recognize the experience as being inherent to the developmental phase of the team, which will naturally wane as the team moves to the next phase of its life cycle.

Individual and team resilience

If we want our teams and organizations to be successful in achieving our goals, as leaders we will need to be able to weather many storms and be agile in the face of change and challenges. Understanding the inter- and intrapersonal dynamics that help us to develop resilience is therefore key to our success.

What is resilience, and how do we nurture it in ourselves, one another and our teams? Resilience is often talked about as if it is a static (does not change) and global (always there or not there) internal factor within an individual. In fact, resilience is something we learn and develop through relationships and experiences. It does not constitute a straight line of growth and is a dynamic factor in our lives. Resilience grows when we feel scaffolded, supported and valued in our relationships, and when we have experiences that help us to feel a sense of agency, success and meaning. When our relationships scaffold our skill development, support us to try new things and comfort us when inevitably things sometimes do not work out, we feel held and 'good enough' despite the challenges. Our endeavour is valued rather than the value being placed on the outcome alone. This is sometimes known as a 'growth mindset' (see Chapter 2) that sees the purpose of actions as being the endeavour and attempting rather than necessarily the succeeding, because an inevitable outcome of trying new things, being creative and stretching ourselves is that things will often not work out as planned. But this experience helps us to hone our skills, knowledge and eventual achievement. So, the purpose of the endeavour and the action is the important part (see the discussion of 'intelligent failure' in the section 'Different types of failure' in Chapter 2).

When we experience feeling *connected* with others, we start to feel more confident and capable, and we eventually internalize the support, comfort and message of being 'enough' that the relationship gives us. Hopefully we have had this experience in our family relationships, with partners or with friends, but if not, our working relationships can provide this for us, perhaps for the first time. But whether we have had this feeling of connection with others or not, it is important that our working relationships are supportive and scaffold our learning, as discussed in Chapter 1. Supportive relationships help us to develop a sense of confidence in ourselves and our ability to achieve our goals and try new things, and let us know that we are okay when things go wrong. *Self-confidence* enables us to 'give things a go' when there is no guarantee of success, and we are pushing outside of our comfort zone. It is linked to us developing a good sense of self-worth that is not tied to outcomes. We feel capable and able to cope with challenge and stressful situations despite them being difficult: 'This is really challenging for me and yet I can still do it'; 'I have coped with stressful situations before and can draw on that in this situation.'

Having a clear sense of *purpose* also helps us to be resilient. Being clear about what we are doing and why keeps us focused when things go wrong, or when we find ourselves in challenging situations. It helps us to make difficult decisions and avoid becoming side-tracked, and helps galvanize us as a team in our shared purpose. Our values and key purpose may be slightly different from those of our colleagues, but generally we will have overlaps and some shared purpose that brings us to the work we share. Exploring this as a team can help colleagues to feel more connected and tolerant and promote a sense of belonging within the team. Arguably, being *agile*, flexible and able to embrace change and recover from difficult times comes as a result, but being agile and flexing our skills and behaviours according to the context and individuals we are relating to is fast becoming recognized as a key characteristic in resilience and performance. However, the pressures and demands within our work and personal life can lead to us feeling a sense of isolation, aimlessness, fear and paralysis, as individuals and as a team. These contradictory feelings lie on a continuum that we can move along in either direction, depending on the context, our relationships and our responses. For example:

- *Isolated:* 'I feel like it's just me, everyone else is okay', or, at the other end of the continuum, *connected:* 'I have people there to help me when I need it.'

- *Aimless:* 'I don't know what I'm doing', or, at the other end of the continuum, *purposeful:* 'I know what I'm doing and why I'm doing it.'

- *Fearful:* 'I'm scared and think that I might fail' to the other end of the continuum, *self-confident:* 'I am good enough to do this and believe that I can.'

- And lastly, *fixed:* 'I struggle to adapt when things don't go as I expect', or, at the other end of the continuum, *agile:* 'I can flex and cope if something changes.'

The Resilience Iceberg

The Resilience Iceberg (adapted from Changing Minds UK, CMUK) is a helpful analogy to support us and our teams to think about the factors contributing to our individual and team resilience at a particular time and over a period.[2] If we think of an iceberg, under the water it is unsafe– we are frequently reactive, closed off and trying to survive. Above is psychologically safer – more open, we can be proactive and have the potential to thrive. Here we facilitate the development of

---

2   See https://changingmindsuk.com/performing-well

resilience. Below the surface, icebergs are frozen, barely change and represent deeply held, core fixed beliefs that can limit resilience development. Issues and problems are not seen or spoken of. We remain closed off and in our own world and experience. We are reactive to events that are challenging instead of being proactive and strategic. This all chips away at our confidence and increases our anxiety. We can then become more fixed and potentially reckless in our risk-taking behaviour and attitudes, and all this means that the qualities associated with resilience are harder to reach.

Above the water, where it is open, more accessible and psychologically safer, we can be proactive to shape our beliefs, helping us move along the continuum in the desired direction, increasing our individual and team resilience. Relationships that are supportive, allow constructive challenge as well as care, and encourage team members to contribute their thoughts as part of an open and psychologically safe system in which we accept, connect and reflect, allow people to feel *connected, purposeful, self-confident* and *agile*, qualities that develop resilience.

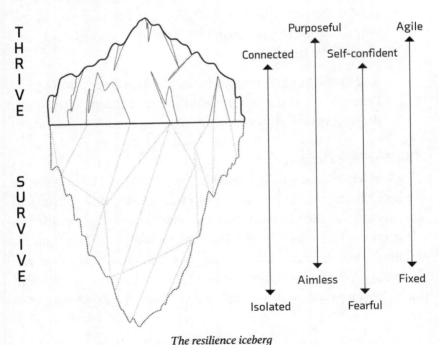

The resilience iceberg

Inevitably we all bob under the waterline at times due to a particular event or multiple stressors. No one sits above the waterline all the time, just as we will all get pulled along the Boundary Seesaw at times. Understanding these key characteristics of resilience can really help us to reflect on what is pulling us below the waterline and how we might, as individuals and as a team, nurture more of the characteristics that help us to be more resilient: 'How can I build closer relationships with others, and seek support when I might need it?' 'What opportunities do my team have to connect (both formally and informally), and how could we build on this?' 'What would help my team to feel more supported and supportive of one another?' 'How can we develop a clear shared sense of purpose and hold that in our minds to help us navigate difficult events?' 'How can we boost our own and our team's confidence?' 'What do we need to try?' 'How do we acknowledge great work or endeavour?' 'Can we share skills and scaffold one another to give things a go that may be a stretch out of our comfort zone?' 'Can we enhance agility in the team and our thinking?'

TEAM TASK: THE RESILIENCE ICEBERG

Draw an iceberg on a piece of flipchart paper. Discuss in small groups where each person thinks the team is currently on the iceberg (for each of the four continuums), and why. Be curious about each other's responses to the following questions:

- What is impacting (currently or historically) where you think your team might be sitting on the iceberg for each of the four continuums?

- What helps/would help your team to stay above the waterline?

- What might lead you to sink below the waterline? Or what might have led you to sink below the waterline in the past?

- What does it tend to look like in the team when you have sunk below the waterline? What do you notice? What behaviours tend to play out?

- What helps your team to feel self-confident and competent, especially when times get tough?

- What gives your team a clear sense of purpose – working together towards a vision, with shared values and a clear strategy?

- What helps your team to feel connected – within their teams and the wider service – feeling understood and heard, that they belong and that they are able to ask for help when they need it?

- What helps your team to be agile – to flex and adapt to changing situations and embrace change?

This exercise can develop a greater team understanding of the strengths, challenges and potential threats that the team might face, how the team might respond (or has previously responded) to challenges, and what could potentially be put in place to start to build greater team resilience in the four key areas. From this, a team resilience development plan can then be made, to support the team to buffer against any potential threats they may face in the future. It is worth coming back to this plan and ensuring it is still relevant to the team and adapted to any changes in context.

Summary

Having a better understanding of, and being able to recognize and name, the interpersonal dynamics at play between people in couples, groups, teams or organizations, can help us, as leaders, to promote more positive dynamics and mitigate unhelpful ones. As leaders, our ability to reflect on our own pushes and pulls in relationships is key if we are to get the best from our relationships with our team members and colleagues. With our teams, we do not need to fully understand the origins of the dynamics we see play out, but an ability to recognize them, name them and bring curiosity about them can bring these dynamics into the light. In turn this allows us (and our team members) to have more agency over these push/pulls in our relationships with our colleagues and our clients. We can avoid some of the pitfalls or at least recognize when we are in them. We can reflect on whether certain behaviours and feelings are expected due to the context of our team in itself or in the wider cultural context. Parallel processes can be observed and named, allowing us to be less reactive and avoid replaying unhelpful thoughts and feelings at varying levels of a system.

Increasing our understanding of interpersonal dynamics increases our agency as leaders in achieving our goals and delivering good practice as individuals and as a team. One of the key factors that shapes the dynamics of relationships, our learning and our experience is language. In the next chapter we will consider how the language we use, what we do and do not communicate, and how we communicate, all influence our leadership and our team.

References and recommended reading

Bloom, S. L. (2011) 'Trauma-Organised Systems and Parallel Process.' In N. Tehrani (ed.) *Managing Trauma in the Workplace* (pp.159–173). Abingdon: Routledge.

Bloom, S. L. (2013a) *Destroying Sanctuary: The Crisis in Human Service Delivery Systems*. Oxford: Oxford University Press.

Bloom, S. L. (2013b) *Creating Sanctuary: Toward the Evolution of Sane Societies* (Revised Edition). Abingdon: Routledge.

Bloom, S. L. (2013c) *Restoring Sanctuary: A New Operating System for Trauma-Informed Systems of Care*. Oxford: Oxford University Press.

Hamilton, L. (2010) 'The Boundary Seesaw Model: Good Fences Make for Good Neighbours.' In A. Tennant and K. Howells (eds) *Using Time, Not Doing Time: Practitioner Perspectives on Personality Disorder and Risk* (Chapter 13, 181–194). Hoboken, NJ: John Wiley & Sons Ltd.

Karpman, S. (1968) 'Fairy tales and script drama analysis.' *Transactional Analysis Bulletin 7*, 26, 39–43.

Microsoft (2022) *Great Expectations: Making Hybrid Work Work*. Work Trend Index: Annual Report. www.microsoft.com/en-us/worklab/work-trend-index/great-expectations-making-hybrid-work-work

Tuckman, B. W. (2001) *Theories and Applications of Educational Psychology*. New York: McGraw Hill.

CHAPTER 5

Language and Communication

This chapter explores what psychological approaches tell us as leaders about the power of language and communication (both verbal and non-verbal) in defining what we choose to talk about, how we talk about it and how others receive our messages, and how important this is within the organizations we lead. We consider how self-awareness and self-regulation are key to optimizing our ability to communicate well with our teams and our organizations. We think about common communication challenges, and how to use communication optimally to support healthy relationship development. The chapter also discusses conflict and debate, and how to get your message across well.

Language is something that is central to all our learning, perspectives and assumptions as humans. If we go back to the work of Lev Vygotsky (an influential psychologist who studied child development), he viewed social and cultural interaction as central to our development, and saw language as the most important tool of all (Morin 2012). We learn what is important, and what our culture and society values, through language. We learn judgements and values from what others say to, and around, us. Language plays a crucial role in scaffolding our learning (social learning, cognitive ability and understanding). However, in addition to language, the way that words are conveyed (emotional tone, body language, non-verbal communication) is also highly influential.

Social constructionism

Social constructionism is a theory that proposes that knowledge and the meaning underlying it are constructed within our social groups, through communication. What is talked about and how it is talked about conveys certain meanings (such as the value or importance of the topic, or how other people may feel about it) and influences the language that we use and how we make sense of the world around us. Our cultural assumptions and expectations in particular are also constructed through language. Ideas and constructs can change across time and between cultures because they are subjective understandings. Some examples of subjective understandings might be around what is seen as 'attractive' within a culture, what is typical parental behaviour or what a working day should look like.

Whether something is named and spoken about within a group of people or a team (e.g., an issue, a challenge, a concern) has a significant impact on the ability of an individual member to name and discuss it further, either within or outside the original group. When something is labelled or named, it brings with it the ability to consider it as something that exists, which can allow further discussion and the development of a shared understanding within a group. For example, when we shared the concept of the Boundary Seesaw in Chapter 4, this has provided you with the concept and language to discuss these dynamics, how they occur and how they affect you, your work and your clients. You can then discuss these dynamics and concepts with other people, in different contexts, at a deeper level, and take the information back to your teams for reflection.

Language can intentionally or unintentionally promote inclusion or exclusion

As language and its associated meaning are created within social interactions, and how language is used can differ between groups, it can naturally have the impact of making an individual feel included or excluded. A typical example is the use of acronyms. Have you ever been in a meeting where there is a long discussion about something where a particular term or acronym is used, and you do not know what it means?

EXAMPLE OF LANGUAGE INADVERTENTLY EXCLUDING PEOPLE

When Toby[1] first joined the senior leadership team within a previous role, he sat in a two-hour meeting where an acronym (let's say EBN) was used. The way that this was discussed within the group suggested that it was of utmost importance and had great value – therefore Toby felt foolish that he did not know what it meant and assumed that it was something that he should be aware of. He spent quite a bit of the meeting trying to work out what the acronym could stand for, and whether he could be mishearing what was being said, while nodding his head and trying to remain feeling part of the group. He later found out that it was a sporting term, which he never would have known or been able to guess.

We might naturally use expressions that we hear all the time within the groups in which we work, assuming that others will understand them, but people outside those groups (such as members of the public who may be stakeholders), or even members of the group, may not in fact be familiar with them. Alternatively, the words that we use may have different connotations for other people. We may use language that is neutral to us, but to others, it could offend. Therefore, with language it can be useful to:

- Consider the words and language that we use, and the potential meanings for others.

- Explore other people's understandings of the language we use in our workplace – does the language have similar or different meanings for them?

---

[1] A made-up name, for purposes of anonymity.

- Be open to exploration and challenge around language.

- Think about any language, terms (such as clinical terms) or acronyms that we use that may be jargonistic or not understandable to others – consider how to make these more accessible, or how to use simpler language that is likely to be more understandable and less exclusionary.

- Be kind to yourself. We might get things wrong sometimes, but if we remain open to learning and challenge from others, we can greatly improve our communication skills, enabling others to feel more included.

- Think about how to promote this culture, within your team and organization, around the use of accessible language, and check out understanding to ensure everyone feels included.

- Give people the benefit of the doubt. People see things differently and interpret specific language differently depending on their associations with the word. So, there is a balance between challenging and accepting difference and good intent.

Dominant narratives

When thinking about how language can be used to influence, it is important to consider how dominant narratives are created. How we make meaning of an event or experience is heavily influenced by the dominant social and cultural discourses that we are exposed to. We develop dominant stories about ourselves, others and the world, and these are shaped by the social messages that we get. Individuals who have 'power' due to their relationship with us (e.g., the impact of parental narratives on their children), their hierarchy (e.g., teachers within a primary school), their fame or their demographic group can have social capital, which means that they can significantly shape the social discourse. Individuals and groups can sometimes take advantage of this social power, and society can also inadvertently enable this. For example, there have been big concerns over the past few years about the impact of significant, famous male figures who are promoting misogynist and violent views to young boys through social media. Often the dominant, more negative narratives that are promoted can have strong (although often false) arguments, a 'smokescreen' of words, and can give inaccurate 'facts' that are difficult to challenge due to the way that they are told (as if they are factual, evidence-based information). Accurate information is often mixed in with inaccurate information and inflammatory language, which makes it harder for listeners to discern where the truth lies. For example, issues about males being the victims of domestic violence are quite rightly raised as something we should be aware of and talking about. However, the way this is presented, and the language used, often disguises that fact that domestic violence disproportionately affects women and girls, particularly serious and fatal domestic violence. Sometimes the issue may be raised and used to dismiss the concerns about violence against women and girls, rather than as a connected issue worthy of consideration and action.

The dominance of a narrative within a social group also makes it very difficult to challenge, as this would make the individual an 'outlier'. For example, if you were in a room of people who strongly believe in gun ownership, you might find it hard to speak up and challenge that narrative about gun ownership, due to a fear of being dismissed, criticized or put down, or perceived as an outsider, knowing that there is a strongly believed argument within the room that is unlikely to change. As we discuss in Chapter 9, you might make a quick judgement based on interpersonal risk and decide that it is not worth speaking up to challenge it. Furthermore, if you were to express pro-gun views yourself, you may then receive some reinforcement (such as praise, support or engagement) from the group, which may strengthen this dominant narrative for both you and them. It therefore becomes very reinforcing to go along with a dominant narrative and risky to challenge it. We may therefore consciously or unconsciously dismiss contradicting perspectives to reduce the perceived threat and maintain the status quo.

When dominant narratives are not challenged, but are instead reinforced by those who believe in them and others are not willing to challenge them, they can appear more attractive and understandable and be taken as fact within a group or culture. Once certain explanations or interpretations of events have been prioritized, and have formed a dominant narrative, information that counteracts those understandings is often dismissed. This is known as confirmation bias, as our brains tend to look out for information that fits with (or 'confirms') our dominant beliefs, and we are more likely to dismiss information that contradicts it.

We know that as humans we can tend to be drawn to conform, as this is easier and makes social relationships more comfortable, promoting harmony and a sense of belonging. Therefore, challenging these narratives can be hard to do. When deciding to challenge these more dominant views, it can often be helpful to find our network and other people with similar views to ourselves or who value challenging discussions, who might also be wanting to make a change.

Saeed Atcha MBE DL, CEO of Youth Leads UK: Challenging negative narratives about young people

Saeed was born of Indian heritage and grew up in the North of England. At the age of three, he was placed within foster care, where he remained (although moving between different foster families). He officially left care at the age of 25 but moved out of care himself at age 21. During his early years, school was one of the few constants that he had, and he picked up the role of running the school magazine, which he enjoyed.

When Saeed was 15 years old, he was struck by how newspaper headlines often talked in a shockingly negative way about young people. He decided that something needed to change. After arguing with a teacher that afternoon, leading to Saeed losing the role of managing the school magazine (as the teacher thought he should focus on his schoolwork instead), he decided that he was going to set up his own magazine with friends. He was passionate about the potential in young people and changing the narrative to a more positive one, particularly around young people with disadvantage, such as those who have been through the care system.

To do this, Saeed reached out to the CEO of O2 via a letter

explaining what he was planning to do, and why. The CEO saw potential in Saeed and his idea, and offered some financial support and a business mentor to help get the project off the ground. Saeed then set up *Xplode Magazine* when he was 15, a magazine run by and for young people, allowing them to take ownership and create more positive narratives about young people and challenging the more negative ones that had dominated newspaper headlines. The magazine is now part of a larger charity, Youth Leads UK, where Saeed serves as CEO. It is published on a quarterly basis with different young people taking a lead on every edition. Since 2011 Youth Leads UK has supported over 20,000 young people with skills development, social action and mentorship opportunities.

Saeed was honoured by Queen Elizabeth II for services to young people and the community in Greater Manchester in 2019. He holds the distinction of being the youngest person ever appointed as a Deputy Lieutenant of Greater Manchester, and his expertise has been sought in capacities such as social mobility commissioners and as a trustee of youth-focused charities (Generation, Education & Empowers, and Migrant Leaders), and he is also a non-executive director at Bolton at Home, where he contributes to the housing sector's governance with a focus on community and social justice).

How to debate or challenge well

It can be tricky to enter into a discussion when you know that the people you are talking to have opposing viewpoints to you. Sometimes, as humans, our 'go to' is to think about how we can convince them that our view is the correct one by stating facts or telling them why their perspective is wrong. We may enter the conversation passionately stating our points and attempting to dominate the discussion. However, there is a danger that when we use these methods of asserting our view, it can lead to further polarization in thinking, defensiveness and a sense of disconnection. So, in this section, we consider how to have a debate and challenge views without unintentionally causing further division. Here are our top tips.

Stay curious and open

Try to remain curious, listening to what other people say, asking questions about how they see the situation and why, their underlying beliefs and what the argument means to them personally, and try to understand where their understanding might have come from. As the other person will be viewing the debate from their own life context, understanding this more fully can help us to take this into account and address it as part of the discussion. It can be useful to hold in mind that more than one viewpoint (even if they seem opposed) can be true or have relevance at any one time, so where we can more fully understand the different possible ways of viewing the situation, this can help us to come up with a better shared understanding.

Things are rarely black and white, and there is often overlap. When we acknowledge this, it can bring people towards us on the continuum rather than pushing them further away (which can polarize the debate even more). It might be that you even agree with parts of their argument, and where you do, it is okay to acknowledge this. For example, 'When you said X, I can see how that might impact Y.' One way to be able to acknowledge what someone else has said while still promoting your understanding is to use 'both…and', that is, 'Yes, that is true, *and* this still needs to change.'

Be aware of non-verbal communication

A large part of the way we communicate is through non-verbal behaviour. Our non-verbal communication has the potential to put the other person on edge, or make them become defensive, even before we start to talk. Or it has the potential to make someone feel more at ease and more willing to talk through things with us, and to be more generous in their interpretations. Our tone of voice is also important to consider, as if it seems to be at odds with what we are communicating, this can feel jarring to the listener. If we come across with an angry, aggressive or defensive tone of voice, it will impact the way that our words will be interpreted (they are more likely to be interpreted with negative intent, for example). To demonstrate how powerful this can be, perhaps try saying a simple everyday phrase (e.g., 'What do you want for dinner?') to someone you are close to, using different tones of voice (e.g., calm, excited, frustrated, angry), and see how they react.

Use storytelling

As described in Chapter 8, we know that when we tell stories and create meaningful narratives with emotional impact, it can help the listener to understand us and our viewpoint better, thus making a stronger argument. Although we might believe that facts can be convincing, which they can be when used sparingly, we know that humans are more drawn to meaningful stories to make sense of things rather than hard data.

Consider how to construct your argument

Prior to entering the discussion or debate, it can be useful to think about, and write down, the key points that you think are essential to get across, so that the other person can more fully understand your position. There are a whole host of different ways to do this, but one that is commonly used within university debating is the SEXI method:

- *Statement:* What is the point you are trying to make?

- *Explanation:* What are the beliefs behind this point?

- *EXample:* What is a clear example of this/the impact?

- *Importance:* Why is this particularly important?

If you are using this to advocate for something to happen, it might be helpful to add an 'R' on the end to detail what you are asking for in a clear, concise manner:

- **Request:** What exactly are you asking for? (Include 'what?', 'when?', 'how?' etc.)

For example:

Young people's views have not been considered within this policy document (*statement*), as there has not been time available for a full consultation involving young person representatives and groups (*explanation*). Where young people's views have not been included previously, such as within the service design, this led to important considerations being missed, such as how young people would access the service, which subsequently led to delays and had a financial impact (*example*). Including young people's views within this policy matters because they are the main users of the service, and they will therefore be able to provide a wider perspective on what we need to consider to make sure that this policy works (*importance*). I would therefore ask that we allow an additional month's consultation period, from today, to allow time with young people representatives and groups around the new policy, before it is finalized and progressed any further (*request*).

Communicating well with your team

There are several things that it can be useful to be aware of that can elevate your communication skills as a leader, including being self-aware and regulated, adapting your communication style depending on who you are communicating with, and being an engaging communicator.

Engaging and inspiring communication

Within our Leadership Training, we often ask attendees what makes an 'engaging leader'. Although there is a range of responses, and often lots of discussions and debates, a few key themes come through:

- Leaders who are fully present in the conversation – they are tuned in to the people they are communicating to and with, and appear fully immersed in the interaction.

- They give enough time to the communication to show that they think that it is important (they do not seem distracted or ready to rush out the door).

- They show empathy and understanding of the audience, perhaps talking to the experiences in the room, or asking questions and listening to the answers. They communicate skilfully and convey interest in what their audience communicates, but also that this is important to them.

- They are enthusiastic and may celebrate the person or team they are communicating with in a genuine way, recognizing skills or achievements.

- They convey a sense of being 'in it together' with their audience.

- Their body posture is open (ideally not sitting behind a desk), and they appear quite informal in their interactions (lessening the power dynamic or sense of hierarchy).

- They appear to have good self-confidence (although not overly self-confident to the detriment of others) and feel comfortable being themselves.

- They show some appropriate vulnerability, but not too much (see Chapter 6).

Therefore, being 'engaging' does not mean that you need to have lots of skill and experience of public speaking or communicating in groups; it just means that you need to be present with others, fully immersed in the conversation, interested in them and empathic to their needs. The 'people' factors here are essential.

Adapting your communication style

When communicating with both individuals and groups, it can be useful to know your audience and adapt your communication style accordingly. For example, in Chapter 6 we talk about personality profile 'colours'. How you view the world and what your preferred ways of working are can impact what kind of communication you might value the most. Obviously, a personality profile only gives a snapshot of that individual, so the best option, if you are going to be communicating with them regularly, is to talk about how you can best communicate together. However, if you are having to think quickly about how to adapt your communication styles, here are some tips to use as a rule of thumb.

Several personality profiling tools used in the workplace are based on two of the 'Big 5' personality dimensions, namely the 'Extraversion/Introversion' dimension and the 'Agreeableness' dimension which rates the degree to which the individual is focussed on relationships as opposed to tasks. These two dimensions cross to make up 4 behavioural preferences. Each behavioural preference is associated with a colour on the tests.' High Agreeableness is labelled 'People focused', Low Agreeableness is 'Task focused', Extraversion is 'Outward focus' and Introversion is 'Inward focus'.

TIPS FOR COMMUNICATING WITH PEOPLE WITH DIFFERENT BEHAVIOURAL PREFERENCES

Red (task, outward focus):

- Clear and direct

- Provide key information only

- To the point – concise

- Action-focused – link to outcome or goal

- Avoid waffle

Blue (task, inward focus):

- Clear and direct

- Provide all the relevant details

- May want time to think through before responding

- Written, detailed follow-up may be useful

Yellow (people, outward focus):

- Communication in person preferred

- Focus on connection and creativity

- Opportunity to think together on the spot

- May find too much detail tiring – may lead them to shut down

Green (people, inward focus):

- Connect first and check in

- Space for informal communication as well as task focus

- Empathize with their position

- May need to be encouraged to share their view, especially if it differs from others

When you are about to communicate something important to a colleague or your team, it can be helpful to spend a little time planning what you are going to say, where and how. This gives you a chance to think about the key messages that you want to get across, consider how these might land, and how to get the best out of your communication. Where appropriate, it can also be useful to talk to a trusted colleague and run through what you are planning to say, to get their perspective and feedback. There is a danger that sometimes we might feel fairly confident and think that that we have it in hand, but then, when we open our mouths to speak, we end up saying something that we did not expect, we become derailed and go off on a tangent, or we notice that the team are reacting in a different way than we expected, which can lead us to react unhelpfully to them in the moment. We can end up causing more fear and anxiety within the team if we have not thought about our communication first.

Emotional self-awareness and self-regulation
Being self-reflective, having emotional self-awareness and knowing how to self-regulate are all important skills to help us to communicate more effectively with others, especially when we are in a leadership role.

When we can have good emotional awareness and are aware of how we are feeling moment to moment, this can help us to know what we need to get the most out of a situation. It can be useful to check in with ourselves regularly and certainly before communicating with our team, and consider how we are feeling emotionally, what thoughts are in our mind and how our body is feeling. For example, it might be that when we take a moment to check in, we notice something we were not aware of earlier, such as we might be feeling tense in our shoulders or we might notice some heaviness in our body.

If we can tune in with how we are feeling, it can help us to know what we need. As we know, emotions can be quite clear communicators when we listen to them. We then might need to up- or downregulate so that we are 'feeling okay' again. An example of upregulating would be doing something to increase our energy levels and feel more connected, if we are feeling heavy, disconnected or spaced out. This might include, for example, going for a run or fast-paced walk, getting a drink, listening to some energetic music or talking to someone about something we are passionate about.

An example of downregulating would be doing something to lower our energy levels and feel calmer again if we are feeling hyperactive, panicked, overwhelmed, angry or distressed. This might include doing something that we find soothing, such as listening to a calming podcast, going for a leisurely walk (or a faster walk to burn some energy off), regulating our breathing, eating something crunchy, doing some slow stretches or having a cold drink with ice.

When we can bring ourselves back to a more regulated emotional state, it can create a more optimal state of mind to allow us to be more skilful in our communication as a leader.

The impact of dysregulation/regulation

When emotionally dysregulated	When in a regulated, balanced state
More likely to be chaotic or overly emotional in communicating	Able to look rationally at information presented and make good, sound decisions
Might unintentionally dysregulate the people around us/our team, as they pick up on our emotional state	Can be flexible and agile and respond to information as it comes along
Not able to think things through clearly or make sound judgements	See things more clearly/see the bigger picture
Struggle to see the bigger picture	Provide emotional containment to others, and set a calm, but energized, emotional tone within the team
More focused and rigid in thinking	
More likely to see things as a potential threat	More in control of how we react and respond
Find it harder to tune in to others or the relational dynamics in a room	Act in a way more aligned to our values
Feel drained and exhausted, which others may be able to pick up on	Improved emotional intelligence (including tuning in to others)
	More creative ability
	Conserving energy – generally feeling better

RECOGNIZE – REGULATE – ACT

- *Recognize:* Recognize your emotional response and how it is affecting you.

- *Regulate:* Take a moment, breathe/go for a walk, use regulation strategies.

- *Act:* When you are feeling regulated, think about how to act skilfully.

Your early warning signs and triggers

Have you ever been in a situation where, for example, a colleague sends you an email asking a simple question and it really irritates you? I mean *really* irritates you. What has happened probably merits a 3/10 feeling of frustration at most, but for some reason, you want to throw your laptop

145

at them or swear (i.e., more of a 9/10 response). Where has this extra '6' come from? We sometimes talk about the concept of an emotional bucket that we all carry around with us. When we are going through stressful experiences (at home or work), it is like we have more water in our bucket. After a while, these stressful experiences (water) start to build up, and then it doesn't take much for our bucket to overflow. It can be useful to think about the main things that tend to fill your emotional bucket, both inside and outside work, and what you tend to carry with you. Then, what are some of the things that tend to trigger an emotional response from you, or lead your bucket to overflow?

What kinds of things lead to you feeling stressed, overwhelmed or frustrated? Are there things that happen at work where you could predict that they might affect you emotionally? Are there ways that you could prepare in advance for these experiences? If you are starting to struggle emotionally, what might you and/or other people around you notice? These are not always obvious. When you can identify your early warning signs, this can help you to catch them when they start to happen, which can cue you to do what you need to, to feel okay again. You might also want to discuss these with others close to you, such as a partner or close colleague, so that they can check in with you if they notice them.

Helping you to emotionally regulate

It can be helpful to work out what helps you to regulate more generally within your life – for example, how can you switch off from work? How can you connect with those close to you? How can you make sure that your basic needs (food, sleep, exercise) are met? What can help you regulate in the moment at work? What helps to bring your emotional arousal level up if you are feeling flat and disconnected? What can help to quickly bring your emotional arousal level down if you are feeling overwhelmed, anxious, distressed or angry?

Setting the emotional tone

As discussed in Chapter 4, we know that emotions are contagious, so what you are feeling will automatically affect the people around you (we 'catch' each other's emotions). As the leader, you have a significant influence over the overall emotional tone of your team, which can have a big impact on team cohesion, effectiveness and performance. Therefore, it is important to be able to tune into or sense the emotional state of the team, and recognize whether it is aligned to where it needs to be. This is commonly talked about as being a *thermostat* rather than a *thermometer*. A thermometer measures the temperature of the room (or team) and reacts to it, whereas a thermostat sets and regulates the temperature to create the optimal emotional environment for what the team needs at the time.

Because emotions are contagious, when people are within a group their emotions can spread quickly. People who did not feel particularly strongly about something at first can start to feel a particular way by being around people with strong emotions surrounding a particular topic. When people express their emotions to others, they themselves can also start to feel them more intensely. Therefore, as a leader, it is useful to recognize how emotions can play out, and become reinforced, within group environments, so stay attuned to the emotional tone of your team and try to gain a greater understanding of the emotions that are being expressed (as your team will be communicating something important).

To do this, you might use your observational skills, have informal discussions with team members, and check in with key people within the team to learn about their understanding of how the team currently is emotionally, both as a whole and as individuals. This is sometimes called a 'team temperature check'. When you have a good awareness of where your team is at, you can then choose which emotions you want to bring to certain situations, to set the emotional tone. For example, you might want to bring a sense of confidence and stability when you notice that the team are feeling anxious and struggling with self-doubt. Or you might want to bring some energy and connection into the room when you can see that people are feeling more disconnected or flat. If you notice patterns within the team (e.g., the team feeling flat and disconnected mid-week), you might want to try to address this through adding a team ritual or activity during key times (e.g., mid-week) to reset the emotional tone.

This could be an opportunity to be proactive rather than reactive by way of connection, energizing conversations or playfulness.

Despite this, we want to acknowledge that it's important that communication from a leader needs to be meaningful, and not always positive. Where there are problems and challenges, these should be acknowledged, not ignored, and ideally addressed. Failing to do so can be invalidating for people experiencing these difficulties. There is a balance to be had. We find that a team that overplays the positive constantly has the potential to be as dysfunctional as a team that does the opposite.

Communication in a crisis

When a team or organization is going through a particularly difficult time, colleagues often look to the leader for guidance, support and direction. In fact, we know that human nature means that we often look to the 'leader' to better understand a situation, how safe/risky it is, and to know how to react. When we look at the person in charge to see how they appear and react, to help us judge the situation, this is an aspect of 'intersubjectivity'. For example, if we are unsure about a situation and we glance at our leader and see that they are anxious and tense, we know that it is something to really worry about, whereas if they look genuinely calm and relaxed, we might feel more confident, too, in knowing that it is not too serious or it will pass. 'Genuine' is an important term here because if it appears that the leader is trying to hide their underlying emotions, this could lead us to worry even more. This therefore means that at times of stress it is particularly important for the leader to be self-aware, and to self-monitor how they communicate with their team, both verbally and non-verbally.

Often when we are leading a team through difficult times, it can be hard to know what to say. Sometimes leaders choose to say little until things calm, as this can feel safer. However, the danger of this approach is that it can lead to 'unproductive uncertainty' (Furr and Furr 2023, p.46), where colleagues are feeling stuck and fearful, or they may start to 'fill in the blanks' and create their own understandings of what is going on. This can be incorrect and potentially damaging. It can lead to the team losing direction and focus, and therefore no longer working effectively, becoming more disconnected or chaotic. It could also lead to someone else within the team starting to 'step up' and attempt to lead, which can create confusion and fragmentation.

TIPS FOR COMMUNICATION IN TIMES OF CRISIS

- *Self-regulation:* Your team will likely look to you, as the leader, to know how to react. If you can remain calm within your communication with the team (and use your own support strategies to help you do this), it will let the team know that you are in control, and that you are thinking carefully about the way forward. If you can work on your self-regulation at these times, you will also be more likely to think and make decisions in an effective way too. Being regulated and calm allows you to share appropriate vulnerability with the team, and this can help you to connect with them and where they are currently at (see Chapter 6).

- *Over- (rather than under-) communicate:* Communicate early and often, to ensure that your team know that you are taking the ever-changing situation into account and will update them when you can. Regular communication helps the team feel more confident in the leader.

- *Dialectical communication:* Sometimes it may seem that two, somewhat opposing, statements could not possibly be true at the same time. Yet, the nuance of human life is that they can both have validity. Instead of this being an 'either...or' situation, we call it a 'both...and' situation. Recognizing this can help us to understand one another and examine the nuance of the topic. It can lead to more honest communication without 'all or nothing' thinking: 'It is true that cuts have added pressures for us over the past few months, *and* in the future we are going to be thinking about how we can use more efficiently the resources that we have.'

- *Drawing on past learning and experience:* Bearing in mind the team and organization's story (see Chapter 8), it can be useful to reflect with the team about past challenges – what helped them to overcome these – to think about the team's resilience and their ability to get through difficult things, and to remind them of what helps.

- *Link back to the 'why?':* At times of crisis or stress it can be helpful if your narrative as the leader can anchor the team to remind them 'why' (see Chapter 3) they do the job that they do, and the impact that it can have.

- *Giving clear direction:* At times of crisis, people will often look to the leaders for clear direction and guidance. Even if you are a leader who tends to consult with their team about decisions, there may be times when you need to step in and give clear direction. Your perceived confidence (even if you are not feeling it inside!) will be felt within your team.

- *Think about challenges as an opportunity for learning and development:* When teams can see challenges as something that will inevitably arise and that can help them to build their skills, experience and resilience, this can help them interpret the challenge differently. The team can consider how they might approach the challenge, seeing it as a potential problem to solve together. This can help them to be able to address and resolve the challenge in a meaningful way, although this obviously needs to be pitched appropriately. It can be an opportunity to make slight tweaks, or to try something quite different to normal practice. Bringing the team into these discussions can help in generating a sense of control and agency.

Communication pathway challenges

Caroline Aldridge, who is a social worker, author, speaker, trainer and practice educator, drafted a diagram that she named the Pit of Inaction Model.[2] She initially came up with it to describe some of the challenges that can arise with communication within large organizations, although she recognizes that this can apply to a range of organizations, and she has had feedback from many contributors within health, social care and education highlighting their recognition of these issues. Her model is quite self-explanatory, and we are sure that it will resonate with many readers. It shows how often so much time within large organizations can be taken up with ineffectual meetings, such as talking about things that end up going nowhere (often with no one present who has the 'power' to action things) and undertaking audits or writing reports that are not going to be read, with decision making getting stuck between higher levels of the system. This leads to nothing really ever changing, and fuels feelings of resentment, frustration and often conflict.

Therefore, it is essential to think about how communication works, or does not work, within your team or organization. Perhaps map it out and share it for comments/thoughts with your team and with people at all levels of the system. Invite their feedback about what is or is not working. It can be helpful to ask yourself:

- Where does communication work well? Where is it effective? Which factors support this?

- How does our communication fit with our overall vision and values? How could we improve and move closer to these?

- Where does communication get stuck, and what are the blockers?

- How does communication filter down, but also up, the organization?

---

2   See www.learningsocialworker.com/single-post/the-pit-of-inaction-my-thoughts

- Does our communication meet the needs of the staff team, and also the clients we are trying to support?

- How could we make our communication more meaningful and efficient?

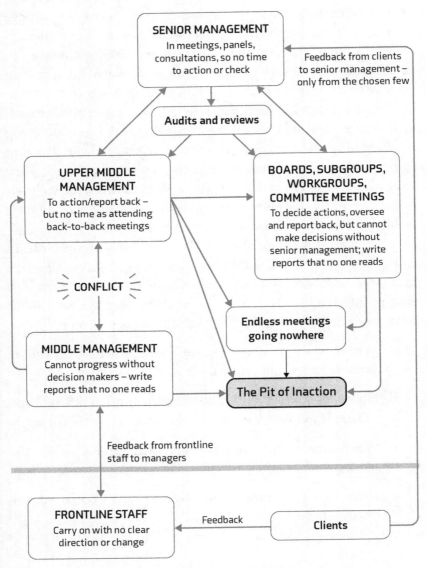

The Pit of Inaction Model

SOURCE: ALDRIDGE (2023)

Timpson Group's Cut the Crap committee

The Timpson Group set up a 'Cut the Crap' committee in 2022 to 'help reduce complexity' within their business. They reviewed all the meetings, forms and processes within the company to see which were really required and which could be disposed of. Then they aimed to reduce the number of communications so that only those that were effective were retained, thus saving time and energy on unnecessary communications. The committee remains strong and continues to meet every few months. We spoke to Janet Timpson (Director of Happiness at the Timpson Group) who told us, 'The ethos is "don't have meetings for meetings sake, and don't provide reports or do a particular job if it isn't necessary and people don't need it." This avoids creating more work for everybody concerned.'

TEAM TASK: CUTTING DOWN MEETINGS

If you want to do this yourself, one way would be to look at all meetings held within your organization and do a quick audit to work out which ones are viewed as useful, which could be made more effective, and which could realistically be dropped. A more drastic way would be to delete all meetings out of the diary, to find out which ones really need to happen, and which have perhaps just been fillers.

Summary

In this chapter, we have considered good communication as a crucial skill of a psychologically responsive leader. This involves understanding the influence of language, cultural and dominant narratives, and how these can be used (intentionally or unintentionally) to include or exclude. It is important as a leader to build an awareness of your own emotional state moment to moment, and to self-regulate before engaging in important communications with your team. We have discussed your role as a leader in recognizing your team's emotional tone, the complex interplay of contagious emotions and how to bring your team to a more optimal emotional state. We have also explored what an 'engaging' leader means, and how to communicate thoughtfully and effectively and to support your team through a crisis. Within this chapter, we have also started to reflect on the importance of ongoing development of self-awareness in leadership, with a focus on your own emotional state, pulls and needs. In Chapter 6 we will build on this further, by considering the importance of vulnerability and recognizing what it feels like when we are feeling too emotionally exposed and start to 'armour up'.

References and recommended reading

Aldridge, C. (2023) 'The Pit of Inaction.' In C. Aldridge and E. Corlett (eds) *They Died Waiting: The Crisis in Mental Health – Stories of Loss and Stories of Hope* (pp.285–288). Norwich: Learning Social Worker Publications.

Bailey, J. and Molyneaux, G. (2008) *The Oxford Union Guide to Schools' Debating* (2nd Edition). https://outspokenela.com/wp-content/uploads/2017/02/the-oxford-union-guide-to-schools-debating-copy.pdf

Furr, N. and Furr, S. H. (2023) 'Toward Uncertain Ability: Leading Self and Others to Possibility Beyond the Unknown.' In D. Dearlove (ed.), *Certain Uncertainty: Leading with Agility and Resilience in an Unpredictable World* (pp.41–48). Hoboken, NJ: John Wiley & Sons.

Morin, A. (2012) 'Inner Speech.' In *Encyclopedia of Human Behavior* (2nd Edition) (pp.436–443). Cambridge, MA: Academic Press.

CHAPTER 6

Vulnerability and Self-Reflection

Developing our skills for self-reflection is central to psychologically responsive leadership, as is our ability to be appropriately vulnerable. This chapter explores what vulnerability means and the steps we may sometimes take to avoid being vulnerable, as well as the essential relationship between vulnerability and courage. The chapter thinks about self-compassion and developing an understanding of what helps us as leaders to feel 'good enough' as being key to our ability to be truly self-reflective. This knowledge also helps us to develop these skills within our team. The chapter then draws from personality-related research to consider leadership 'colours' on a good/bad day, helping us to develop awareness of our leadership strengths, what these may look like if they are overplayed, and our potential blind spots.

What is vulnerability?

What we think and feel about vulnerability is shaped by the cultural narratives we experience about vulnerability within our families, key relationships, community and our wider society. How vulnerability is talked about, modelled and reacted to within our social experience will shape how comfortable we are with the idea of being vulnerable, as well as our direct experiences of being vulnerable ourselves. These cultural narratives about what vulnerability means may change over time or vary between different families or cultures. Cultural assumptions and expectations regarding vulnerability may vary depending on the individual's sex and age, and potentially other characteristics – for example, the possibility of vulnerability being perceived more negatively in men and in young to middle-aged adults compared to women, children or older people. Vulnerability may even be 'projected' onto certain demographic groups, expecting certain people to be more vulnerable than they are, and this can be undermining.

Through our work with organizations and teams, we have noted that most people assume negative associations with the term 'vulnerability'. They mention how as professionals we might talk of a young person or patient's vulnerabilities, that vulnerability is often associated with weakness, and they notice their own negative reactions to the word. However, with further discussion, someone will usually contribute an alternative perspective on vulnerability and suggest that vulnerability may actually demonstrate that someone is comfortable with not knowing all the answers or 'showing they are human'. Soon we are in a rich conversation of the necessity of vulnerability and then the pitfalls of demonstrating 'too much' or no vulnerability at all, both as an individual and as a leader.

It has a significant impact on both the leader and the team's functioning when a leader shows no vulnerability and feels they must present themselves as being 'all knowing', powerful, in charge, unflappable, unemotional and potentially unmovable. These characteristics may be perceived as bringing many positives to the team, although there are many potential negatives too. The leader has set themselves, or may perceive other people see in them, an unrealistic standard of being a human being and a leader. They are likely to struggle to ask for help or seek other people's thoughts and perspectives, due to them feeling they are expected to provide all the knowledge and answers as a leader. The leader may find it difficult to communicate when there are issues and challenges due to their perception that this would suggest a personal failure in some way. They may also fail to connect emotionally with their team members regarding the realities of the ups and downs of life and their work. The team miss out on opportunities to contribute to problem solving, provide their knowledge and develop their skills, therefore removing any chance of enhancing a sense of belonging and shared ownership within the team. The team may find it harder to share their concerns, worries or mistakes, as their leader does not model this as being acceptable, and is sending an unspoken message that expressing worries, concerns and mistakes, or not knowing what to do, is negative. Labouring under the idea that as a leader you should and must be 'all knowing' and 'all powerful' is exhausting, impossible to live up to, and bad for individual wellbeing and also for the development and wellbeing of the team. It causes leaders to feel defensive and highly stressed, and defensiveness often plays out as a stress/threat reaction, as discussed in Chapter 4.

Conversely, a leader who demonstrates a very high level of vulnerability is likely to feel exposed, stressed, anxious and unstable, and their team is likely to feel this too, due to a lack of emotional containment from their leader. Stress and difficult feelings will flow unmanaged through the team and have an impact on morale and performance. Vulnerability without boundaries is not helpful and is not the kind of vulnerability we are talking about here. If we are sharing our innermost personal emotions and experiences without purpose for the team, we are simply emotionally 'bleeding all over them'. So there is a balance to strike here. Vulnerability needs to be authentic and appropriate within the context. It is often useful to think, 'How might my sharing this vulnerability impact the team, either positively or negatively?' There is not one particular point on a continuum that is desirable for a leader, but more a middle ground area, in which the leader may move depending on the needs of the team and the context of the situation.

It may be useful for you to reflect on the contexts in which you feel that showing your vulnerability – such as not having all the answers to a problem, of being open and verbalizing when something feels very stressful and challenging, and needing help and support – could be helpful to both yourself as a leader and also your team. If there is a crisis, what kinds of vulnerability are helpful and unhelpful? If you are going through a really difficult time personally, what kind of vulnerability would you feel is needed and appropriate? If you are feeling significant pressure from your manager and others senior to you, but your team are unaware of this, is it useful to communicate your feelings and situation? And to whom?

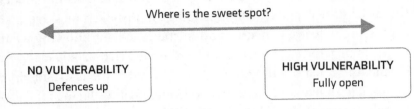

The vulnerability continuum

What is key here is our emotional intelligence. Our ability to recognize and name difficult feelings and challenges is an extremely helpful skill to have as a leader. This allows us to name the feelings that are held in the team, or to explain the challenges we feel in our position as leader. The team will then feel able to talk about difficulties, recognise and express difficult emotions, problem solve together and support one another. But this communication needs to be purposeful. If we are 'emotionally offloading' onto our team, sharing information that raises anxiety and does not serve them in any way, we are slipping to the right-hand side of the continuum and demonstrating uncontained vulnerability. This does not serve our team. However, as leaders we need some safe relationships in which we can share our experiences without censure. This may be a personal relationship, in supervision, or with a mentor or coach. It is important that leaders have spaces to be and feel, to express the reality of their human experience without having to have their 'leader' hat on in that moment. Having this space to talk openly and be understood allows us to feel more emotionally regulated and able to share information with purpose, and helps us to support and contain difficult emotions and experiences within our team. To take such space with people who know us well or have leadership experience (which allows them to understand our position well) is an extremely important part of supporting and enabling ourselves as leaders. Just as parents benefit from trusted friends who are also parents and fully understand when it comes to the challenges and emotional rollercoaster of parenting, the same applies to leading in our work.

SELF-REFLECTION

- Who are your trusted supporters you can lean on in tricky times?

- Who have you got in your 'inner circle' whose opinion you trust and who is able to bring appropriate challenge to you to help your development?

- Do you have regular supervision? Is your supervision internal or external to your organization, and what are the pros and cons of this for you?

- Would you benefit from engaging with a mentor or coach?

Armouring up

When we protect ourselves from any vulnerability, we slip towards the left end of the vulnerability continuum and become defensive. As Brené Brown (2018) suggests, we can put on our armour ready to protect ourselves and potentially attack in self-defence. We become self-protective and often end up 'masking' what is really going on for us, sticking our heads in the sand, avoiding and failing to address the problem. When human beings are defensive, we often deflect responsibility and project blame onto others, potentially trying to make someone else feel vulnerable instead of us, in an attempt to alleviate our own sense of vulnerability. We can become intolerant of vulnerability in others too, becoming harsh or even attacking. Much of this is unconscious behaviour that we slip into when we feel vulnerable and defensive. However, learning to recognize this in ourselves and the contexts in which this is most likely to happen allows us to mitigate the impact of our defensiveness and engage in relationships and behaviours that help us to feel understood, valued and 'good enough', despite a really challenging situation and difficult emotions.

As human beings we also show our defensiveness in our non-verbal communication. Our rate of speech, tone of voice, facial expressions, eye contact, body posture, how we hold our body (facing towards or away from others) and whether we place barriers between us and the other person such as folded arms, a desk or cushion are all shaped by how safe or defensive we feel. Therefore, raising consciousness of these non-verbal communications, checking in with ourselves and ensuring that we align our non-verbal communication with our intended communication with the other person can have a significant impact. If, despite my feeling anxious and somewhat defensive, I manage to control my breathing and tone and show engaged facial expressions, eye contact and open body posture, I can affect the 'feeling' of my communication with the other person. Even if the communication is difficult, I can help manage that difficulty and increase the sense of connection and emotional regulation through my non-verbal communication, as well as aspects of my verbal communication (this is discussed in more depth in Chapter 5).

SELF-REFLECTION

Recognizing the kind of situations that trigger our defensiveness and our 'armouring up' can be helpful self-knowledge that allows us to recognize what we are experiencing, and to take helpful steps to alleviate any negative impact for ourselves and others. Take time to ask yourself what armouring up looks like for you when you are feeling defensive. What might others notice? How does it feel in your body? How do you behave? What might you be thinking or feeling in this moment? How does it affect your decision making? These questions help us to deepen our self-knowledge and catch ourselves earlier when we are armouring up, allowing us to act sooner and potentially learn more quickly.

TEAM TASK: ARMOURING UP

It can also be useful to reflect on what armouring up looks like in your team. What would an observer notice? When does this happen? What plays out in the feelings and behaviours of the team? How is this managed or not? Reflecting on this can help us to pick up earlier when our team are feeling vulnerable and defensive, allowing us to act sooner to address the situation. Having this discussion with our team at a time when we are not experiencing high stress can also be very helpful in raising our team's self-knowledge and emotional intelligence. What do they notice and what do they think helps? Hearing differing viewpoints can be useful in developing our understanding of our team's collective and individual needs, how we can support them and what helps them to support one another.

Courage is underpinned by vulnerability

Brown (2018) argues that contrary to vulnerability being weakness, vulnerability is our greatest measure of courage. She has articulated vulnerability as being when we experience risk, without guarantees, but despite this we 'lean in' and face the challenge. Brown also states that her research has demonstrated that stories of courage are always 'underpinned by vulnerability', which is consistent with our professional experience as clinical psychologists. This may be taking responsibility when things go wrong, pushing ourselves out of our comfort zone to try something new and anxiety-provoking, or taking our first steps to rebuild after a devasting loss, all in the knowledge that despite our endeavours, we may fail. Brown also recognizes the paradox that we often value and take comfort in vulnerability in other people, allowing us to feel connected with them, but resist showing vulnerability in ourselves. However, our ability to tolerate the uncertainty of success, to push ourselves out of our comfort zone and to try something new is arguably a key factor in resilience, as well as courage. This allows us to develop beyond where we were yesterday and where we thought our limits were. Therefore, being able to tolerate vulnerability and uncertainty is key to growth, emotionally, socially and performance-wise. When we cannot tolerate vulnerability and shut it down, becoming defensive, our ability to connect with others, to hold the big picture and think clearly, is reduced. We are surviving rather than thriving.

We hope by this point we have convinced you that the idea that vulnerability is weakness is untrue, and, in fact, vulnerability is part of the human condition and the basis from which we can 'show up', endeavour, learn and thrive. This is also the same for teams. If we want to innovate and be creative in our work, we need to value endeavour and not shame people or projects when things do not go as planned. In order to learn lessons quickly and be creative, we require open and honest conversations. These conversations may be challenging at times – we may need to acknowledge where things went wrong and take accountability, which can be uncomfortable to us as individuals, as leaders, and as a team. This requires supportive relationships within the team. Therefore, the culture of a team is extremely important in creating a healthy atmosphere in which the shared purpose of the work is clear, and team members support one another in their endeavours to take on new and creative projects, activities or roles that are ambitious and stretch the individual and/or team. Failure despite effort needs to be embraced and recognized as an inherent part of development. Scientific advances are made when a team of scientists are innovative and try a multitude of iterations in order to get to the final product, often with many instances of failure and learnings along the way. Understanding this is sometimes known as a 'growth mindset' (the importance of intelligent failure is explored in Chapter 2).

Feeling 'good enough'

Leading is challenging, complex and demanding. Therefore, being aware of how we, as individuals, support our wellbeing and feel 'good enough' despite our flaws, and our 'not knowing' at times, is important and requires reflection. Many leaders talk of feeling like an imposter who will be 'found out' at any moment. Leaders have talked to us about having recurrent dreams of being 'caught out' or even limiting their own careers and opportunities due to a sense of other people being 'better qualified' in some way. We also recognize that when we feel better about ourselves, we can be more open, less defensive, and therefore more accepting of our own vulnerability and fallibility without being derailed by it. Therefore, recognizing our strengths, skills and worth is an important factor in helping us to identify and avoid 'armouring up'.

A good understanding of our own strengths and how we can best leverage these is important, as is understanding our poor behavioural and communication habits. However, it is also important at a human level to take stock of the resources we have that support our wellbeing. This might be current or past relationships, activities that are good for us or meaningful to us, or thoughts and perspectives that help us to feel better at challenging times. Self-awareness is the cornerstone here, and thinking about, noticing and mapping out the resources that help us to feel good enough as human beings and as leaders is time well spent. Here we share our own resources that help us to feel good enough when events are challenging (and also when they are not).

WHAT HELPS ME TO FEEL GOOD ENOUGH, BOTH AS AN INDIVIDUAL AND AS A LEADER?

It can be useful to spend time to reflect on what might help you to feel 'good enough', both as an individual and as a leader. Perhaps jot down some notes or draw out your thoughts.

You may come up with examples such as:

- Feeling physically strong – exercise, gym or taking on physical challenges.

- A specific personal relationship with someone I feel wholly accepted by.

- When I push myself out of my comfort zone and achieve something.

- An old boss/tutor who believed in me and stuck up for me at a difficult time.

- Watching or listening to stories (e.g., reading, film, podcast) that widen my perspective and help put things in context.

- Talking things through with someone I trust.

- Feeling connected with and loved by my pet.

- Reminding myself that self-doubt is a normal part of being a human and does not need to derail me.

- Walking and being outdoors.

If we are to take on difficult roles and challenge ourselves, it is important we learn what helps soothe us and energizes us. It is extremely important, if we want to be a good leader, that we reflect on what we have achieved positively and understand what helps us to 'switch off' after work and absorbs our attention; what helps us to feel connected to others; and what brings us joy or helps us to feel calm and emotionally regulated. Not only are we able to be more honest in our self-reflection when we feel 'good enough', but it also helps us to take on board feedback from others. We can accept the positive feedback without having to dismiss it and can also seek out and hear any critique or developmental feedback without becoming unnecessarily defensive. Feedback becomes part of our learning and growth, both as individuals and as leaders.

Understanding our own strengths and weaknesses as individuals
360-degree feedback
When we come to appraise our work, gaining feedback about our work from multiple sources, including a variety of colleagues, managers and clients, can give us a coherent perspective – 360-degree feedback refers to the collection and consideration of perspectives from individuals in various positions, connected with our work. Our own perspective is also taken into consideration, so we can compare

our perspectives with other people's, and try to make sense of any differences.

Understanding the strengths that we can bring to our roles and our team and how we can truly maximize these strengths is an imperative part of our development as leaders. We can assess what these strengths are through honest self-reflection, and feedback from our line managers and colleagues, from our clients and even from our close personal relationships. All these people will experience us in different roles, engaging in varying modes of communication, and therefore their feedback can really help us to gain a good picture of how others perceive what we are good at. Taking time to seek informal feedback is valuable, and ensuring that regular feedback is gathered for our personal development plans (PDPs) or appraisals is key. Ensuring this feedback is 360 degrees and includes the perspectives of our colleagues, seniors and juniors and our clients allows us to get a full picture of how we are performing and how we are experienced by others within our role. Linking the evaluation questions to the core competencies of the role helps to bring a coordinated approach to how the team deliver their purpose. For example, a core competency may be 'Creative thinking', defined as 'Being playful, creative, and innovative when approaching our work. Being open to new ideas and ways of doing things.' Or 'Good self-management', defined as 'Able to work autonomously where appropriate, manage own time and set boundaries around this. Strong drive and hardworking. Good organizational skills, excellent at problem solving.' Including these core competencies within the 360-degree feedback for our PDPs allows the individual to reflect and receive feedback on how they are meeting these core competencies and informs their PDP.

Psychometric profiling

Some organizations or individuals find it useful to engage in psychometric profiling to better understand the personality and strengths profiles of individuals or the team. There are various tools that provide an insight into our strengths and skills and what we may struggle with or enjoy least in terms of our communication style and approach to our work. We like to use a tool developed by Mindflick called Spotlight[1] with the teams we support, which is described as a 'Powerful and intuitive online personality profiling tool designed to help individuals and teams develop adaptability. Spotlight super-charges coaching conversations about performance, growth, and collaboration by shining light on mindset and behavioural style.'

Spotlight recognizes that humans behave differently depending on the context, that our preferences do not always align with our skills, and that we can also adapt and change. Many personality profiling tools categorize us as a 'type', whereas Spotlight considers our pre-ferred ways of working and behaving. It assesses our Mindset, based on Reward Sensitivity Theory, and our Behaviour, based on whether we are Task- or People-focused, External- or Internal-focused. The blend of the two measures gives a comprehensive overall profile that we have found helps individuals and teams really understand themselves. Spotlight is a strengths-based tool that measures our preferences rather than ability, and helps us to gain an insight into how we set about achieving our purpose, and how these unconscious methods fit with our colleagues' methods of achieving the same. It also gives us an insight into where we might misapply or overplay our strengths so that they turn into potential weaknesses. It helps us in understanding ourselves and how others might experience us, as well as appreciating the value in other people's perspectives and methods of achieving our shared goal.

If you do not have the opportunity to engage in a profiling tool, it can be helpful to take time to think about how you lead on a 'good day' and the pitfalls you can fall into on a 'bad day'. These two are often linked, as we exaggerate our strengths when we are stressed. Or sometimes our strengths and preferences may not be fitting with the context and what is needed in that situation, or with that particular individual. For example, we both prefer clear and direct communication, being goal-focused and driven. However, when this behaviour and communication is not right for the context, such as within a consultation and listening exercise, these preferences can be experienced as 'bulldozing', being too blunt or dismissive.

---

1   See https://mindflick.co.uk/spotlight

Additionally, when we are in a stressful situation, we may be more likely to overplay these strengths and behave in a manner that is too blunt, direct, controlling and dismissive. Understanding this has helped us to get the best from our strengths, while minimizing the weaknesses of our preferences.

Agility and adaptability lead to improved performance

We can be more adaptable to the requirements of the context and the individuals we are engaged with when we have a good understanding of our strengths and what we find more difficult. And this is also true when we recognize our strengths can become weaknesses when they do not fit the context, or we overplay them. As we discussed in Chapter 4, agility is fast becoming recognized as a highly desirable skill in employees and leaders as it is a key factor in improving performance. Nik White discusses the importance of recognizing his own strengths and weaknesses and adapting his leadership style to the context.

Nik White, Managing Partner at Brabners LLP, a leading purpose-led independent law firm based in the UK: Adapting leadership style

I believe there is a balance to strike in terms of leadership style, and it's important to be adaptable. As the pandemic first hit, it was critical to give clarity and reassurance that, while no one could be absolutely certain about what was going to transpire, we were on it, we had things under control and we had confidence, thereby creating a sense of calm, comfort and assurance for our colleagues. So, exuding confidence and giving clarity and direct communication was important in this context. In other contexts, a more consultative, creative and shared approach is needed.

During my time in leadership, I have become more confident in recognizing and being open about not only my strengths but crucially also the things I am not so good at. I have become comfortable to acknowledge and communicate that I do not have all the answers, and to surround myself with talented colleagues and draw on the strengths of others within the team. The key is to be open about our weaker areas as leaders and to recruit, promote and empower colleagues who have strengths and skills you don't have, or that outweigh your own abilities, and who can plug the gaps and make a valuable contribution. Key traits of good leadership are relatability, authenticity and the ability to engender trust, and I certainly think leaders who are uncomfortable demonstrating vulnerability may face challenges with their leadership and relationships with colleagues.

Valuing the perspectives of others and recognizing that individual experience has led to them having differing tactics to achieve the same shared goal allows us, as leaders, to be more tolerant and curious of other people's approaches, reasoning and behaviour. We can appreciate that they might be able to bring a differing perspective to our work and therefore enhance our performance and outcomes. Being able to consider a variety of experiences and perspectives allows us to make the most informed decisions, prepare for and ameliorate challenges, and produce a more comprehensive piece of work. The difficulty is that it makes us comfortable if we surround ourselves with people who think just like us and see the world through a similar lens; however, this narrows our perspective and reduces our performance. So, seeking out and encouraging the sharing of views, creating what Fanshawe (2021) terms 'safe spaces for disagreement not from disagreement', is valuable to us as human beings, as leaders and as teams.

Hearing from people who think differently from us allows us to consider aspects of the subject to which our own experience cannot lead us. Your team can help you to get a balance between being both people- and task-focused, reflecting and doing, being aware and planning for potential pitfalls, managing well when things go wrong, while also grabbing potential opportunities, taking calculated risks and celebrating achievements. As individuals, we are likely to have preferences for one or two of these perspectives over the others. Being aware of the strengths of other people in our team allows both us and our team to gain from their strengths and not be limited by our own strengths and weaknesses as the leader. In order to achieve this, we have to help create a culture that supports the sharing of ideas, the appreciation of varying perspectives and the tolerance of disagreement. It can therefore be helpful to share our preferences, strengths and potential overplays with our team, acknowledging where we might need support, as this can subsequently lead to others being more willing to share their own preferences and challenges.

Where we do not have a culture of tolerance and interest in varying perspectives, we can easily become surrounded by, or only hear from, people who think like us and who only reinforce, and fail to challenge, any of our thinking. In a team or any group of people this can turn into 'group think' and a dominant narrative, where the members hold a narrow view of a problem and the solution to that problem while ignoring complexity and nuance. Our ability as leaders to be self-reflective, to have humility in understanding both our strengths and our limitations, and the capabilities of other people, is key to our valuing the perspectives and communication of our colleagues (see Chapter 5).

Summary

No individual is bullet-proof. We are all physically and emotionally vulnerable. We all have strengths and talents as well as areas of falli- bility. Accepting our human vulnerability and seeing it as the basis for courage is analogous to a 'growth mindset', as discussed in Chapter 2. A growth mindset recognizes that failure is inherently part of crea- tivity and endeavour, and therefore by accepting this reality (without an undue negative response) we give ourselves the freedom to push ourselves and to try things beyond our current skill set. Similarly, by accepting that vulnerability is part of the human condition and also the basis for courage, we can acknowledge our difficult emotions, our frailties and our significant challenges. Instead of viewing vul- nerability as a hinderance to our wellbeing and performance, it can, in fact, enhance it.

If we assume as leaders that we need to be all-knowing and all-present, this can have a negative impact on our wellbeing, and also on the development and agency of our team. Recognizing our own strengths and those of our colleagues, recognizing when we need to adapt our leadership style to enable others to take the lead, and taking time to understand ourselves, our unconscious drives and our patterns of behaviour, can help us to be the best possible leader of ourselves and of other people.

In order to be vulnerable, we need trust, trust in ourselves and in others that we are safe or at least 'safe enough' to be authentic. In the next chapter we will unpack what 'trust' means, and why trust and integrity are central factors in successful leadership.

References and recommended reading

Brown, B. (2015) *Daring Greatly: How the Courage to Be Vulnerable Transforms the Way We Live, Love, Parent and Lead.* New York: Penguin Life.

Brown, B. (2018) *Dare to Lead: Brave Work, Tough Conversations, Whole Hearts.* London: Vermilion.

Fanshawe, S. (2021) *The Power of Difference: Where the Complexities of Diversity and Inclusion Meet Practical Solutions.* London, New York, New Delhi: Kogan Page.

Morgan, J. (2023) *Leading with Vulnerability: Unlock Your Greatest Superpower to Transform Yourself, Your Team, and Your Organization.* Hoboken, NJ: John Wiley & Sons.

Sinek, S. (2017). *Leaders Eat Last: Why Some Teams Pull Together and Others Don't.* New York: Penguin.

CHAPTER 7

Integrity and Trust

This chapter discusses the interplay between psychological notions of competence, humility and trust within leadership. It explores the impact on individuals and teams when they feel trusted and are able to trust in their leader, as well as the impact of a lack of trust. Some psychological models of trust are explored, and we then consider behaviours associated with the different components of trust and how to develop these.

Our ability to feel trust in relationships is key to our social connections and our social, emotional, moral and even cognitive development. Without experiencing trusting relationships human beings remain in a defensive, hyperaroused state of threat, often known as 'fight, flight, freeze or flop'. If we are defensive and cannot trust in relationships, there is a significant barrier to us learning and benefiting from those relationships. This learning can be emotional, social or cognitive, but when our brain is in a defensive threat mode, our higher-level brain functions, such as reflecting, perspective taking, impulse control, planning, attention and focus, centred in the cerebral cortex, are not accessible (or are less accessible) as our biological and emotional reserves are focused on our survival.

Dan Hughes is an American clinical psychologist who noticed that children who have experienced frightening and traumatic parenting learn to mistrust people and relationships, and this significantly impacts their attachment relationships with others, how they see themselves and how they experience the world (Hughes 2017). When we are supporting parents and families, we understand the importance of building trusting relationships, and this is a key focus of our work. When working with any group of people, be it families, couples, teams or organizations, the same is true. People need to feel trust in others and to feel trusted to get out of their biologically driven 'threat response' and use their higher brain functions to develop, feel more at ease, feel good about themselves and feel able to take on challenges.

Competence, humility and trust

When we think about good leadership, we might think about many different characteristics, such as communication, building relationships, specific skills, encouragement, etc. But at its heart, it could be argued that leadership comes down to three key characteristics: competence, humility and trust.

- *Competence* might be understood as our ability to undertake the requirements of the role such as understanding the work and having the skills to communicate this and the ability to have positive relationships with colleagues and clients to enable other people and to fulfil the purpose of our work.

- *Humility* allows us to recognize the limits to our own skills and the value of other people's perspectives and strengths, forgiving their weaknesses and supporting them to develop these or collaborate with others who have this skill (discussed further in Chapter 6).

- *Trust* is a key ingredient in a team performing and working well together and meeting their objectives. Our colleagues should feel able to trust in us as leaders to lead the work and care about them as individuals, and for us to also show trust in our team, delegating and giving our colleagues opportunities to lead and develop.

Michael C. Bush (equity visionary), in his 2019 Ted Talk, suggests that 'trust and respect' are important in creating 'happy' employees. But what does this mean? He highlights three key areas that can support the building of trust and respect within the workplace:

- *Enabling employees to make decisions and have agency in service of the team or organizational purpose.* When employees are given a sense of agency within their workplace, this can help them to feel trusted, valued and respected. For example, organizations such as the Timpson Group allow their shop managers independent decision making regarding the running of their shops. They show trust in their colleagues to know what their clients need and how best to meet those needs. Where leaders can give agency and show trust in their colleagues, this gives them a sense of independence, responsibility and accountability. Employees can be creative and flexible in their approach to understanding how they can deliver their service using the strengths of their team and understanding the local needs of their clients. As discussed in Chapter 1, giving people the opportunity to take responsibility, to take the lead and be creative, can be an incredible way of developing new skills and a commitment to the purpose and organization. When we say we trust our colleagues but maintain control and fail to listen to their perspectives, our actions do not match our words, and so it is unlikely that they will feel trusted, despite what we say.

- *Fairness between employees.* What is good for the goose is good for the gander. Nothing erodes trust faster than a perceived lack of fairness. If employees are given special treatment due to their position, sex, race (or any other characteristic), relationship with the boss, etc., inevitably trust will be compromised. If specific and untypical provision is needed for an individual, it is incumbent on the leader to communicate clearly to the team, in an appropriate way, why this decision has been made. Companies that pay their male and female employees differently, despite being the same grade, or leaders who overlook transgressions or give special privileges to favoured colleagues will have poorer perceived levels of fairness (and therefore trust) in the leadership. A lack of fairness will also breed discontent and resentment between staff.

- *Listening.* What we mean by listening is not just putting on your best 'listening face' but being truly curious about someone's perspective, and being open to being influenced by it. If we cannot influence and be influenced, then trust in relationships suffers and the point of communication becomes obsolete. This does not mean you need to change your mind, but changing your mind has to be a possibility. Colleagues need to perceive that their opinion matters, and that it has the potential to shape team decisions.

Taking time to think about the characteristics that help you to trust someone can inform you, as a leader, of the characteristics you can bring to your colleagues to nurture trust. Think about the relationships and dynamics within a team. What are the behaviours and rituals of the team? What can you bring as a leader to your team to build connection that will support the building of trust too? Having a shared sense of purpose, as we have discussed in several of the chapters within this book, is a key way to help build and maintain connection within any group of people. In a team that takes time to explore its shared purpose and values, colleagues are more likely to trust each other, even when they disagree about something major. The fact that they have explored and understand their shared purpose, and trust in this consensus (this is crucial), allows them to give one another a little 'wriggle room'. They are more likely to be curious with each another when they disagree and have a more generous interpretation of the other person's actions or motives. This leads to a greater sense of trust between colleagues.

Trust takes time to build through all the actions and rituals we discuss in this, and other, chapters. It is built in small actions and interactions every day, over a period of time. However, trust can also be eroded quickly if there is a significant breach of trust without leaders timely addressing what has happened, how and why it occurred, and recognizing and validating the experiences of the employees in response to this breach of trust. Leaders who choose to deny the breach or ignore it are only deepening the problem.

The impact of feeling trusted

We ask our Leadership Training attendees to think about a time they have felt trusted and reflect on how that affected them, emotionally and behaviourally. Our attendees often talk about feeling 'believed in' and how this can improve their confidence and/or their willingness to take on a challenge. It encourages them to take accountability and strive to perform well to meet the task. In contrast, a lack of trust can often have the opposite effect, with employees failing to take accountability and responsibility. They have less motivation to push themselves and take on a challenge, as, due to a lack of autonomy, the challenge is not linked with them as an individual and their performance to the same degree. Not feeling trusted can also lead to pushback and sometimes sabotage, even if this is unconscious rather than purposeful. Being trustworthy is not enough to create a culture of trust; we need to demonstrate trust in others too.

Charles Feltman's definition of trust and distrust

Charles Feltman defines trust as 'Choosing to risk making something you value valuable to another person's actions' (2021, p.9). This definition inherently links the aspects of vulnerability and trust together. We cannot put trust in someone without making ourselves vulnerable to some degree. It is when this trust is reciprocated with a recognition of the belief the other person is placing in us (and the vulnerability they are experiencing to do so) that meaningful bonds can be made between colleagues. Feltman defines distrust as 'What is important to me is not safe with this person in this situation (or any situation)' (2021, p.11). When we distrust, we are defensive and self-protective. This leads to the kind of threat responses we have discussed throughout this book, and when we feel under threat or are hypervigilant for threat, we are likely to engage in defensive actions such as withdrawing, withholding, attacking, arguing or ignoring. We become reactive rather than proactive. Being proactive involves considering multiple sources of information (some of which may be contradictory), holding the bigger picture and various perspectives to make a considered plan of action. When our threat response is active, we act instinctively on restricted information, as survival requires fast thinking and decisive action. When we are reactive and our threat system is activated, we 'armour up', which compromises communication, feelings of safety, rational thinking and other higher brain functions. Therefore, trust is further undermined and distrust increases.

Feltman identifies four key aspects of trust:

- *Care:* Showing care for the interests of others and not just our own interests.

- *Sincerity:* The importance of actions and words aligning – saying what we meaning and mean what we say.

- *Reliability:* Keeping promises and commitments; being someone on whom others can depend.

- *Competence:* Having the skills, knowledge, capability and resources to deliver the work/role.

Dennis and Michelle Reina's three C's of trust

A further model of trust, developed by Dennis and Michelle Reina (2015), suggests that there are three key areas that can lead to the building and breaking of trust within teams:

- *Trust of Character (also known as 'contractual trust'):* Care of one another, and a belief in each other's good intentions and that people will act as they say that they will, in line with agreed expectations (thus proving reliability), with clear boundaries and team agreements around behaviour.

- *Trust of Communication (also known as 'trust of disclosure'):* It is safe to talk directly and openly with one another, giving candid feedback to support each other to grow and learn (seeking feedback from each other), and working through concerns together. There is a sense of collaboration within the team. It is safe to own up to and acknowledge mistakes.

- *Trust of Capability (also known as 'trust of competence'):* A belief in the ability of others to do their role well, with recognition of the particular skills and competencies of different individuals within the group, allowing them to contribute for the good of the overall team. The team use the strengths of one another and seek each other's perspectives when making decisions.

By encouraging and nurturing these behaviours within a group, as leaders we can support the building of trust within our teams and organizations. Alternatively, when these are broken, this framework can give us the language to be able to talk about what has gone wrong, and how we might need to build up trust again in a particular area. This can then enable us to be specific and purposeful in our language, and support us to consider with others how to address these concerns.

These models of trust, and the elements that help create trust, can really help us to understand at a more cognitive as well as emotional (and sometimes intuitive) level what helps human beings to build trust, and how our communication, actions and routines can either build or diminish trust.

When I (Gill) was a newly qualified clinical psychologist, as part of my role, I worked within a paediatric diabetes team. I would attend outpatient clinics for the children alongside the team's paediatrician, dietician and specialist nurse. However, most of my work involved offering support sessions for the children alongside the specialist nurse, Joyce.[1] Over time, Joyce and I got to know one another and developed a trusting relationship. We built trust in our empathic care for the young people and their families, our competence in our individual expertise of psychology and diabetic care, and in a shared sense of purpose to support the children's physical and psychological wellbeing. This allowed us to develop a sort of 'double act' within our sessions, where (for example) I would ask questions and sometimes challenge Joyce, holding the child's perspective and experiences in mind. The trust we built not only allowed us to enjoy working together and push each other to find the most helpful and

---

1   A made-up name, for purposes of anonymity.

creative solutions for our patients, but also helped the children to feel understood and cared for by the paediatric team.

These models recognize the importance of integrity in their summaries of trust. Feltman names integrity *Sincerity*, and Reina and Reina use the term *Trust of Character*. Both models highlight the importance of our actions and words aligning, and being honest and open in our communication, even when this is difficult to do. This relies on our being able to have difficult conversations, and recognizing and admitting when we make mistakes or when things could have been done better. While we recognize that integrity is a key factor in building and maintaining trust, it does not mean we will always get things right as a leader, and inevitably, at times, we will fall short. But recognizing when we do, and acknowledging it, can help to repair trust too, as long as this is infrequent and not recurrent.

TEAM TASK AND/OR SELF-REFLECTION: TRUST

- What are the behaviours, communications and rituals of a leader and team that have a good level of trust?

- Thinking about Charles Feltman's four definitions of trust, how could you, as a leader, 'live' each element of building trust?

  - What would you need to do?

  - What processes could you put in place to support this?

  - What can you do immediately, and what can you work towards?

Trust and the brain

As you will have gathered throughout this book, we think that understanding our neurobiology and how this affects our sense of safety, wellbeing, communication, reactions, development, skills, etc., is helpful in raising our awareness of the neurobiological influences over our behaviour and emotions. Understanding these neuro-biological systems helps us to increase our agency over them, to make intentional choices about our behaviour and emotions, and to be proactive rather than reactive.

Current neuroscience research suggests that we have two neuro-biological systems related to trust. The first supports and promotes feelings of trust, safety, connection and creativity, while the other is designed to keep us safe and survive (fight, flight, freeze or flop), by being vigilant for threat and generating thoughts and emotions such as defensiveness, suspicion and fear. These systems have distinct areas of the brain and utilize different hormones that act as neuro-transmitters. Oxytocin is associated with trust in social relationships. It helps us to bond and connect with others, and reduces the impact of stress hormones such as cortisol, thereby reducing our perception of threat.

As we have discussed within this book, when we are more relaxed, we can bring our prefrontal cortex 'online', which fosters our reasoning, impulse control, planning, attention and focus. When we are stressed and feeling distrust, we are anxious, fearful, angry, hypervigilant for threat, and our limbic systems are activated. This is associated with higher levels of cortisol and testosterone. Our bodies unconsciously reserve our energy and resources for our survival and the associated lower-level brain areas (brainstem and limbic system), and our prefrontal cortex and higher-level functioning is 'offline'. This threat response network makes very quick and instinctive deci-sions to keep us safe, and it reacts in an unconscious way.

It may be that we distrust easily for a minor reason and then our confirmation bias leads this to snowball. Of course, in some situa-tions this is necessary and keeps us alive and safe, but this system can often be over-sensitive, and we may end up being triggered into distrust unnecessarily, without using our rational mind. However, we can make conscious decisions to calm our threat neurobiological network through emotionally regulating ourselves and using discus-sion with a trusted and co-regulating friend/colleague to explore our thinking and feelings. This brings our 'trust network' and rational abilities (prefrontal cortex) back online and releases oxytocin, helping us to hold all the emotional and rational information. Calming our distrust/threat system, activating our trust system and using the skills of our prefrontal cortex also helps others to feel trusting and safe, because, as you know by now, emotions are contagious.

Summary

In order for human beings to push themselves, to be creative, authentic and self-reflective, we need to have trust: a sense of trust in one another and in ourselves that we can be 'sufficiently safe'. This safety is not absolute, and it is always relative. However, if we feel 'sufficiently safe' as leaders, it enables us to lean into relationships to get the best from them in terms of support and learning. It allows us to push ourselves out of our comfort zones, to be creative and take calculated risks, because we know that even if things go wrong, we will be supported and we will survive. Our trusted people will pick us back up again, dust us down and help us to put one foot in front of the other.

Integrity is an inherent part of trust. When our words and actions align, when we are consistent in our behaviour and acknowledge when we make mistakes, others are able to trust in us. Trust and safety are biological needs in order for us to develop and perform well. As we explore within the next chapter, when we understand and articulate our own leadership story, or the story of our team or organization, we can acknowledge the experiences and impact of both challenges and triumphs. This can help others understand and build trust in us as leaders and in the team.

References and recommended reading

Brown, B. (2018) *Dare to Lead: Brave Work, Tough Conversations, Whole Hearts*. London: Vermilion.

Bush, M. C. (2019) 'This is what makes employees happy at work.' The Way We Work, TED series. www.ted.com/talks/michael_c_bush_this_is_what_makes_employees_happy_at_work

Fanshawe, S. (2021) *The Power of Difference: Where the Complexities of Diversity and Inclusion Meet Practical Solutions*. London, New York, New Delhi: Kogan Page.

Feltman, C. (2021) *The Thin Book of Trust: An Essential Primer for Building Trust at Work* (2nd Edition). Bend, OR: Thin Book Publishing.

Hughes, D. A. (2017) *Building the Bonds of Attachment: Awakening Love in Deeply Traumatized Children* (3rd Edition). Lanham, MD: Rowman & Littlefield.

Reina, D. S. and Reina, M. L. (2015) *Trust and Betrayal in the Workplace: Building Effective Relationships in Your Organization* (3rd Edition). Oakland, CA: Berrett-Koehler Publishers.

CHAPTER 8

Narratives: Personal and Organizational

If you want me to accept your vision, or convince me of an idea, tell me a story. Give me the context, the history, the emotions along the way, and let me know how it all fits together.

This chapter focuses on the importance of stories and storytelling to human beings, and all aspects of leadership. It applies psychological understanding to storytelling, demonstrating that storytelling helps us to build meaning, emotional connections and greater self- and other-awareness, to reflect and learn from our histories, and create shared ways forward. The chapter then provides a framework to develop your own leadership stories, as well as resources to co-create a shared narrative with your team.

The history of storytelling

Humans have told stories throughout history as a way of communicating meaning – stories of who we are, our contexts, making sense of things that have happened and our potential futures. Storytelling is natural for us, as our brains are hardwired to find patterns and search for potential meanings in our everyday experiences. This then helps us to create heuristics, or understanding 'short cuts', which we then apply in our everyday lives, helping us to make quick judgements and decisions on what to do and how to react. Stories are clever ways of communicating key messages to other people, such as what is 'wrong' or 'right', how humans behave (or how they 'should' behave) or about potential dangers or what is important. In short, we understand the world, life, relationships and ourselves through internal and/or external stories, which are either conscious or unconscious.

Building connection

It helps to create connections quickly when we tell stories with, or to, other people. We attune to stories in the moment and 'feel with' the storyteller, as we hear and try to make sense of their narratives based on our own experiences and understandings. Storytelling creates the opportunity to bring people together where they may recognize that they have shared life experiences, perspectives or key values. Where narratives are co-created, or individual stories are discussed around shared events or experiences, this can also start to create a 'collective identity' and a deeper sense of belonging.

Creating meaning and understanding context

We make sense of ourselves and others through speech. We know that meaning is constructed through our social interactions and communication, and this shapes us, our values, and how we see and understand ourselves, other people and the world more generally. The dominant stories of our culture, family and about ourselves have an integral influence on our understanding of the world and our experiences. However, listening to the stories of others can also create opportunities to develop greater empathy and diversity of perspective. Stories can help us to develop understandings behind the behaviour and actions of other people, which can enable us to then see the situation differently. They can help us to better understand why people might believe certain things, or may act in a particular way, and can challenge some of our underlying assumptions or biases. Stories help us to see that there could be multiple ways of viewing the same situation or experience, providing an opportunity to find commonality, but they can also be a way of exploring and accepting some of the different views and experiences within a group.

Previous research and theory have proposed a range of benefits to life story narration. For example, positive and negative events may be integrated with self-identity, which can help to form a more stable sense of self and a greater understanding of how we have developed over time. Narration also increases the coherence, richness and structure of a story, starting to put things into a temporal order and helping the individual to look at causal factors and turning points, as well as explanations for events.

A healing process

When we go through difficult or traumatic times, either as an individual, family or team, we are often left with disconnected, inconsistent or even incoherent narratives. Extreme stress impacts our brain's ability to process memories, and therefore often leaves us with fragmented, emotional memories. So, when a person has unresolved stress-based memories, their ability to speak about the experience in a coherent and rich way may be impaired. The more psychologically distressed the narrator is, the less coherent the narrative will be. A first step for these individuals may be to name the stressful experience, and to have the opportunity to feel validated and listened to by another. When a stressful event remains un-narrated, the person may be unable to process the experience and make sense of its potentially traumatic or contradictory parts. Being heard by another individual, and that person reflecting the story back to the narrator in an accurate manner, can play part of the process of moving on from the difficult experiences.

Disclosing difficult life experiences to others has also been suggested to create more 'distance' from the experience, making it less intrusive and more a remembered experience with reduced negative emotion, and a better understanding of the event. This is likely because accurately naming emotions and feeling understood helps us to feel more emotionally regulated. Emotions are largely right hemisphere-based in our brains and connected with the limbic system in our lower brain whereas language is more left hemisphere and higher-brain structure-based. So, we are connecting different areas of our brain to understand and process the experience, rather than this remaining an emotional and visceral experience.

Often trauma or stress can lead us to move away from other people and can fuel disconnection within teams and systems. However, we know that to truly heal and process what we have been through, we need to come together to reconnect and rebuild relationships, and to make sense of what has happened (bringing meaning and purpose). Within this process, we can also choose how we want to frame the story – from a story of despair, hopelessness and powerlessness to one of hope, resilience and courage. If we look at the research around post-traumatic growth, we know that talking with other people and making sense together can be an important way of being able to move forward with a greater understanding of what happened, but also of ourselves and others.

Shared journeys

It can help us to make meaning of what we have been through when we create narratives and understandings about our histories. When we do this, we are selective in the information we choose for the story, which is typically what we see as important. We then place the information into a sequence, with a beginning, a middle part and an end, within a time frame. Certain themes or perspectives are prioritized within these stories to communicate key messages. Our narrative interpretation of what has happened can then be used to make meaning of the world that we live in, and can influence how we choose to act in the future.

When this process is undertaken within a group setting, we can co-create stories, which can be told and retold, with different parts being highlighted or deepened over time. These can then create a sense of shared history, community and belonging, and a shared journey.

Storytelling in leadership

Within leadership, we use stories and narratives much of the time – whether it is at the start of a meeting to explain the context of what we are about to share, or whether it is discussing from where an organization originated. There are often stories of courage, of purpose, of realizations, of big challenges and coming together. We can use stories to communicate who we are today as a team, or organization, and where we came from. Team or organizational stories can help employees to feel part of something much bigger than themselves, and to see their place within the story.

Stories bring purpose, meaning and context. When we ask for more information about an occurrence within work, or we feel that there has been poor communication, often we are not wanting solely more factual information (although this can be useful too); we want to know about the rationale behind decisions, what the plan is going forward and from where this has originated. We want to truly understand more about what is happening, and where it fits in the team or organization's (or wider system's) story. Therefore, the leader's ability to communicate through storytelling or rich narratives can help people to feel included and informed.

Storytelling can help us to gain an understanding of what we, and others, have been through. This may include how we have been able to cope and get through really difficult events and experiences, which may make us feel more confident to confront challenges in the future. When we tell stories that develop over time, this can also help us to make links between things that have happened previously and our, or other people's, future actions or beliefs. At the time we may not see this clearly, but when we have the chance to talk them through with someone else, we can deepen our understanding. Your team/organization's mission, vision and values statements are integral to you creating and telling the story of your organization, both for individuals within the organization and for those outside.

For example, when we spent some time mapping out an organizational story with some senior leaders, including their roles within it, it became clear that at some stage their work had started to feel more like a chore, and less meaningful. We then spent some time with them unpicking when this change had happened, what was happening around this time in the story, which factors had perhaps led to this change, and how this aligned with their own personal stories and values. This led to a deeper understanding of what was important to them, individually and as a small group, and how the shifts within the organization over time had gradually moved them away from what drove and energized them. Consequently, they were then able to think about what was important to them individually, and as a group going forward, and how to start to move towards this again.

Within this chapter, we will focus on individual leadership stories (your own personal story), the team's story and the overall organizational story.

Individual leadership stories

As a leader, it can be helpful to spend some time reflecting on your own leadership journey. Developing your own leadership stories, and telling these stories, can be a process of making meaning of your life and what have you been through, the key factors and characters that have influenced your journey, and where you are hoping your story will lead. This will give you the opportunity to communicate to others your choices, understandings and why you have made the decisions you have – to increase their understanding of you.

When developing your personal leadership story, you might want to consider the following:

- Which experiences have you been through within your life that you feel have influenced your leadership journey? (And how did you make sense of these?)

- Which experiences have shaped you as a leader? (And how did you make sense of these?)

- What do you think have been your 'turning points'?

- What have been your changes in job roles or employers? How did you make sense of these, and what impact did these changes have?

- What have been your 'key learnings' about life in general, about yourself and others, or about leadership? (And what influenced these?)

- What (and who) has contributed to who you are as a leader? (Influences can be more positive, negative or both.)

- What have you been exposed to in terms of differing leadership styles, and how have these influenced your own practice?

- Where are you heading as a leader – what is your desired leadership story destination? What are your next steps?

We would recommend that you take some time out to do this, and then continue to reflect, further building this understanding and story over time. One of the most helpful ways to do this is to talk it through with someone you are close to and whom you trust, such as a supervisor or mentor. Listeners have an important role in the narration process, as they can prompt narrators to elaborate on their stories, which can bring greater understanding, cohesion and richness. This could be through the listener asking questions, or through developing a relationship where the narrator feels safe to explore and reflect on their story.

Telling our stories – how much to share

We know that the opportunity to tell your story, with engaged listeners, can feel empowering, so there is a danger that you could end up over-sharing accidentally as you get caught up in the story. There is a bit of a fine line when telling personal stories as a leader, wanting to give a little of yourself and show some vulnerability (which can create connection and greater meaning), without over-sharing and leaving the listener feeling burdened, anxious, overwhelmed or 'emotionally exposed'. You might want to consider:

- What is too personal to share?

- Will sharing this be of benefit to the listener?

- Is this helpful to share? Or is this giving information that might be unhelpful or overwhelming?

- What might be the impact of sharing this story? (Good or bad?)

The context is also important to consider when thinking about what to share – who is going to be there? What is the purpose of the gathering? Would sharing this story be relevant and helpful at this moment in time? Or would there be a better time, place and audience?

It can therefore be useful to share your stories with people you trust who are not directly within your team, so that they can help you to work out where the boundaries lie – what to share and what not to share. They can also help you to think about which parts of the stories are important to highlight, which are not important, and how to frame the story. Telling your stories can be extremely helpful when you have the opportunity to practise (and then practise again!)

Team and organizational narratives

Holding and sharing a team or organization's narrative is arguably a key role of a leader, as it is imperative to integrate meaning within all your communication with the team – for example, explaining the rationale behind decisions, introducing and onboarding new staff, and explaining the shared way forward. The team and organizational narratives can start from where the organization or team comes from, their context and why they exist (their purpose and what they are trying to achieve). It can tie in the values and purpose of the organization together with more context to increase team understanding and awareness. One of the biggest challenges that we often hear concerning communication within organizations is that it either does not happen, or when it does, it is full of buzzwords and lacks substance or meaning. When we communicate through stories, we can develop much greater understanding, empathy, togetherness and belonging.

Telling organizational stories can bring clarity. There is often so much going on within organizations that sharing key narratives can help people to see through the noise and understand what is happening, and identify the key messages and parts of the journey. It can also help the team to understand how their role and unique journey fit into the team's path going forward. It can provide space for reflection and 'making sense' of the team's journey, which can enhance feelings of belonging.

There is something particularly powerful about a leader being able to name, and talk through, difficult things that have happened. It can help employees to feel that their experiences of difficult organizational experiences issues are understood, that the leader 'gets it' and is not going to shy away from or ignore difficult things. It can be extremely validating, which can create a sense of being 'in it together'.

It can be particularly powerful when the leader can name some of the views, prejudices, conflict, resentment or challenges that might be hidden/previously unnamed, but that are present within the group. For example, within a social care team, a middle leader was able to acknowledge that staff felt like a new senior leader who had come into the organization was making lots of unpopular decisions that appeared to be against the values of the team. However, this middle leader understood the wider context and had a greater understanding of the motivations behind these decisions and some of the challenges that had led up to these decisions being made, which the staff were unaware of. The middle leader was therefore able to share carefully with the team some context and story around some of the challenges that the senior leader faced within the role. This created greater empathy and acceptance from the wider staff team as they could see the rationale for the decisions, even if they did not fully agree with them.

Different ways of telling stories within teams

There are several different ways of telling stories within teams. They may be shared in an informal way (e.g., over lunch), or it might be that formal time is dedicated to reflecting on the story with the team. You might choose to be the main storyteller, and this can be really helpful as it can show the team that you understand, and it gives an opportunity for you to show some vulnerability and self-reflection, which can create stronger connections with the team. It also shows the team that you hold the narrative and story of the team in mind, and therefore hold this bigger context when decision making. It can help you to be able to name the possible difficulties (e.g., how do we/might we cope as a team when under pressure?) and to think about ways in which to buffer against them and where the team's challenges might lie.

However, when the leader leads on the storytelling, there is a danger that this could invalidate or ignore other stories within the group, leaving people feeling unheard. Therefore, when this happens, it is useful if the leader can open up the floor to other possible understandings or experiences: 'These were some things that have happened that stood out to me. Are there any that I've missed?'

Co-creating stories

We can create space for reflection and the building of deeper connections when we share or co-create narratives within our teams or organizations. Stories can give the opportunity to explore and develop a greater understanding of different views and perspectives of the same, or similar, events, to create shared meaning. This can shape and challenge the views that we currently hold. It can be a way to find common ground within stories. Pulling out the themes of the stories and paraphrasing them can help people to understand better the views of others with similar experiences. Listeners may also recognize parts of themselves or their experiences within the stories, which can lead to deeper shared connections or 'social ties' being formed.

Collaborative storytelling can give us the words to talk communally about our shared experiences and the complexities and challenges. Sometimes 'naming it to tame it' (Siegel and Bryson 2012) is a way to make things easier to talk about. For example, within our team, one of our colleagues called the Covid-19 pandemic the 'shitshow', which was a term that spoke to the experiences of our team members at that time. Therefore, this term stuck within the team from then on.

It can be incredibly powerful when the team's story is co-created, but it also has the potential to be more interpersonally challenging. These discussions can elicit strong emotions, and can intensify dynamics within the team if they are not handled with care and sensitivity. The facilitator needs to ensure that there is space and time for reflection, and for each person to have the chance to take part in the creation of the story. The leader will not be able to know in advance where the narrative will take the group, or what the outcome will be, so will need to trust in the process and allow the group to come to this together.

There are several things to be aware of. First, it is important that those engaging in storytelling feel safe to do so (see Chapter 9). It is also important that this is facilitated well so that all voices are heard, the storytelling is inclusive, and people do not feel excluded or dismissed. In addition, it is important that all stories are listened to and taken seriously, and that there are true attempts to understand them and to check out that the understanding is correct. As part of this process, there might be stories that are uncomfortable to hear, such as ones that might highlight challenges within the team or mistakes that have been made, and it can be tempting to minimize or dismiss these. There may be views and experiences that have not been discussed within a group, so co-creating stories gives the chance to bring these unheard experiences into the room and to create greater understanding of the story of the group as a whole. It can also flatten the hierarchy temporarily in a helpful way, as leaders 'work with' the team to develop the story.

If you are aware that there are some difficult dynamics within the team, or that you might experience some 'pulls' to step in, defend or challenge unhelpfully (although some measured challenge can be helpful at times), you might want to consider asking someone external to the team to help to facilitate these discussions. This will allow you to be one of the team, to step back and hear the stories, as well as adding your reflections. Storytelling is something that can take a bit of getting used to, but once a team is used to creating the time for reflecting and co-creating stories, it can become a big part of the culture.

These are some questions you might want to ask when creating a team story:

- Where did we start? Why was the team or organization formed? What 'problem' were/are we trying to solve? What is our purpose?

- What was happening at the beginning? What was our initial context (in terms of the team, key individuals or wider systems/society)?

- What experiences have we been through as a team that have shaped who we are and what we have become? How have these impacted on us? (Understanding individual stories within this.)

- How have we made sense of our journey or experiences?

- How have these impacted on our beliefs about us as a team, our relationships with others and what we do?

- What are our strengths and resources as a group?

- What makes us unique or different from other groups/teams?

- What challenges have we faced (in the past or more recently), and how did we experience them? What helped us to get through these challenges?

- How do we react as a team when we face challenges or stress or when we are under pressure? What plays out/has played out when we are under stress or threat? (Consider this question with compassion, recognizing that we are all human, and it is understandable that 'things get messy' when we are under pressure; see Chapter 4.)

- What have our key learning experiences been? What learning/understanding do we want to take forward with us?

- What should we do next? What is the next step of our journey?

Creative storytelling

There are lots of ways to be a bit more creative with your co-creation of stories. Here are some of our favourites.

Drawing things out

You might want to work together to draw things out on a board or flipchart. This might include, for example, drawing out a timeline, providing lots of pens, and asking the team to draw out or write words along the timeline to indicate things that have happened that are important to them, and their experiences of each event. Alternatively, you might want to hand out pieces of paper and ask the team to draw or write out their journey over the past year as a group. You could also do similar things with sculpting clay, thinking about changing relationships and additions in the team, and mapping this out through sculptures. We have known a team to do a 'stop motion animation' video of their team's story, which could then be shared with new team members. This allows a playful element to the telling of the team story.

Metaphors and analogies

When telling team stories, you can think through and integrate metaphors or analogies. Common ones, for example, are mapping out a team's journey in a temporal way as if it is a river, marking its inception, the twists and turns, the rocky times, waterfalls, calm and peaceful waters, dark woods, the times when it has flooded, where there have been droughts, etc. One analogy that we have used with teams is the idea of a boat within a stormy ocean, and how, at times, it might be about prioritizing safety and coming together, letting the sail down, and waiting for the storm to pass, while knowing that soon the waters will calm and the sail can be hoisted again.

Team wallpaper

In our conversations on our EVOLVING podcast, Kim Golding (a clinical psychologist) spoke about the idea of using a roll of wallpaper to map out a team or organization's story.[1] Since then, we have used this idea with several teams, including our own.

To do this, choose a roll of wallpaper – ideally one that is patterned

---

1   See https://ddpnetwork.org/library/evolving-psychologically-responsive-leadership-kim-golding

with something that has meaning to the team or that is in the team colours. You might want to do the initial draft of the story on flip-chart paper or a whiteboard. When you are happy with the story (it is 'good enough'), you can transfer it on to the wallpaper. You will probably continue to add new bits, and 'layer' the stories over time.

Use the wallpaper to write (or draw) out the progress of the team, noting anything that felt important to team members, whether this is work-related or personal. The stories and experiences that you add can be positive ones, stories of achievement, new opportunities, fun and silliness, courage and resilience. You might want to mark key changes and the impacts on the team, and when people joined and moved on. It is also important to acknowledge challenges, failures and key learning points, and how these have impacted on the team and their culture and practice.

At times, it might feel too soon to be able to step back and reflect on particularly difficult stories or bigger pictures. For example, it felt quite hard to reflect fully on the impact of the pandemic within the first few months when it was still ongoing. However, it can be added on to the wallpaper at the time, and then reflected on the next time the wallpaper is rolled out. Any additional reflections, understandings or emotional impact can be added at that stage. This deepens the understandings, reflections and stories over time as they are being retold by the group.

The wallpaper can then become part of the team culture, which is brought out at regular times (such as team days) to add the next parts of the story or the team's journey to reflect on the story so far, or to consider where the team will go in the future and what learning it can take with it. It can also be a way of bringing new team members on board, helping them to understand the team stories, history and context, and allowing them to feel a part of it.

Dr Claire Smith-Gowling, Clinical Director of Therapeutic Care: The wallpaper task

Following a period of significant change for my team, I organized a reflective practice session for us to come together and create a shared narrative of where we have come from, where we are now and where we hope to be. We have some very creative team members who asked if we could do some reflections using a creative medium, and I suggested we might be able to use wallpaper to capture some of this process. There was an initial sense of uncertainty about how this would work, but very quickly team members began to mark their reflections, experiences and journeys on to the paper in a timeline, with paints, pens, chalks, glitter and feathers! Without any verbal communication, team members were making sense of their own experiences in the context of others. Everyone's journeys were reflected as horizontal lines across a page, but as the task evolved, those lines connected and reflected experiences that were more shared. Towards the end of the task, team members started to be curious about the stories and journeys of others. There were reflections on individual experiences, but these were made sense of as a group and put together like pieces of a jigsaw to create a shared story. I was surprised by how powerful this exercise was. There was so much curiosity, openness and respect for individual experiences, which held safety for everyone's vulnerability. The team loved it, and have asked that we continue our wallpaper journey in the future.

Summary

This chapter illustrates that through storytelling with your team, as a leader you can create a shared purpose (Chapter 3), utilize your responsive communication skills (Chapter 5), and demonstrate your ability to show some appropriate vulnerability and self-awareness (Chapter 6). We have considered the inherent psychological need for humans to create meaning as individuals and as groups of people. Storytelling enables a leader to either share stories that communicate key messages effectively and in an engaging way, or to support their team to co-create narratives that have the potential to build stronger connections, a sense of belonging and being 'in it together'. Stories help us to articulate and process challenges, build awareness of both ourselves and others, and even 'heal' after difficult experiences.

In order to create space for teams to explore, talk openly and share their own experiences (and gently challenge those of others), it is important that they feel safe enough to do so. Therefore, the next chapter explores how leaders can 'generate' a sense of safety within their teams and organization, in order to create psychologically responsive environments.

References and recommended reading

Collective Change Lab (no date) Systems Storytelling Project. www.collectivechangelab.org/ssi-new

Lieberman, M. D., Eisenberger, N. I., Crockett, M. J., Tom, S. M., Pfeifer, J. H. and Way, B. M. (2007) 'Putting feelings into words: Affect labeling disrupts amygdala activity in response to affective stimuli.' *Psychological Science 18*, 5, 421–428. doi: 10.1111/j.1467-9280.2007.01916.x.

Siegel, D. J. and Bryson, T. P. (2012) *The Whole-Brain Child: 12 Proven Strategies to Nurture Your Child's Developing Mind.* London: Robinson.

Slingerland, G., Kooijman, J., Lukosch, S., Comes, T. and Brazier, F. (2023) 'The power of stories: A framework to orchestrate reflection in urban storytelling to form stronger communities.' *Community Development 54*, 1, 18–37. doi:10.1080/15575330.2021.1998169.

CHAPTER 9

Generating Safety: Creating Psychologically Responsive Environments

In this chapter, we will delve deeper into the concept of psychological safety, from where it originated, and how our understanding of it has developed over time. We will think about what it really means within the health, social care and education workplace and why it is so important, and consider how to build more psychologically safe teams. We will also consider a leader's role in creating the environment to cultivate safety within their team, explore some of the challenges and barriers and think about how to overcome these. This chapter takes a systemic perspective to consider factors that impact positively and negatively on psychological safety, from an individual level right through to a societal level. While we have discussed the importance of safety within previous chapters, we are aware that psychological safety is an essential part of creating high-performing and psychologically responsive environments, which underpins the topics that we have covered so far. Therefore, we decided that a full chapter was needed to fully explore psychological safety in more depth as it pulls together discussions from the various aspects of psychologically responsive leadership we have explored throughout the book. Where we can work to create safety, we can create teams and organizations that can thrive.

The history of psychological safety

You have probably heard of the term 'psychological safety' within the leadership literature, where it is recognized as something that is an important (or even integral) factor for team effectiveness. Although it has been talked about since the early 1960s, the concept became much more prominent following a study by Google, which was described in *The New York Times* in 2016 (Duhigg 2016).

Google was keen to learn which factors, behaviours or work habits would most influence high performance. They initially assumed that if they combined the 'best people', then they would be able to create the perfect team. In 2012, they undertook a five-year study, named Project Aristotle, which focused on what made the 'best' or 'most perfect' teams in terms of effectiveness. Once this was understood it could be replicated and create many highly effective and functioning teams across their own and other business. Project Aristotle studied 180 of Google's teams to try to find out why some teams performed particularly well, while others were left behind. They undertook over 200 interviews with their employees and explored over 250 attributes that they hypothesized could influence team effectiveness.

Google invested in this project with the hope that they would stumble on something that would revolutionize their practice going forward. They brought in several top professionals including organizational psychologists, engineers, statisticians and sociologists. They started to look at the academic literature and research and studied many factors that they thought could influence 'team effectiveness'. This included individual factors (e.g., interests, personality type, what motivated individuals, educational backgrounds, skill set, experience, intelligence) and team factors (e.g., size of team, gender balance, socializing). However, as a lead of the project named Dubey (cited in Duhigg 2016, p.20) concluded, 'We had lots of data, but there was nothing showing that a mix of specific personality types or skills or backgrounds made any difference. The "who" part of the equation didn't seem to matter.' They just could not find any patterns in the data that made sense.

As they continued to ponder over their findings, Rozovsky, one of the researchers, and her colleagues had started to notice that within much of the psychological and sociological research on teams and groups, there was discussion around 'group norms' and their impact (Rozovsky 2015). 'Group norms' can be defined as 'the behaviours and unwritten rules that a group adhere to without much attention' (Edmondson 2018, p.xviii). Project Aristotle then changed its focus, and started to look through the data already collected, but this time looking for 'group norms' within the teams, the 'unwritten rules' within a group that seemed to form part of the team culture.

In 2010, Woolley and her colleagues undertook a study that aimed to measure systematically the intelligence of groups (rather than individual intelligence). They split their 699 participants into small groups, and gave each group 10 tasks to do that required different skills and expertise, for example, problem solving, moral reasoning, ethical dilemmas and idea generation. Their findings suggested that individual intelligence could not be used to predict group (or 'collective' intelligence). However, they did find that when a team performed well on one particular task, they typically seemed to also do well on the others. Similarly, if the team performed badly, they seemed to do this on all tasks, not just one. When they explored further, they concluded that the way that the people in each team treated each other was of utmost importance and a key factor, rather than how they went about the tasks or who was in the group. However, they were able to identify two common behaviours that seemed to be present in almost all of the highly effective teams:

- *Equality in distribution of conversational turn-taking.* This meant that everyone in the team spoke roughly the same amount (even though this may have varied from task to task). They found that when one person, or a small number of people, dominated the conversation, the collective intelligence reduced.

- *(High) average social sensitivity.* This meant the team members were good at 'reading' the facial expressions, tone of voice and non-verbal cues of others, and understanding how they might have been feeling. The team tended to be more effective overall, and the collective intelligence increased when team members were 'tuned in' to how other people in the team were feeling, and noticed when they might have been upset, anxious or feeling left out, adjusting their behaviour to accommodate this. In addition, the less effective teams generally had less than average social sensitivity towards their teammates.

These two behaviours are key descriptors of psychological safety within the research. Therefore, when the Google researchers, led at this time by Rozovsky (2015), discovered this concept, their findings started to make sense, and they could translate these findings directly onto some of the data. Rozovsky and colleagues found five key team dynamics that were present for their most high performing teams:

- *Psychological safety:* Can we take risks in this team without feeling insecure or embarrassed?

- *Dependability:* Can we count on each other to do high-quality work on time?

- *Structure and clarity:* Are the goals, roles and execution plan of our team clear?

- *Meaning of work:* Are we working on something that is personally important for each of us?

- *Impact of work:* Do we fundamentally believe that the work we are doing matters?

Out of these five, psychological safety was viewed as the one that was the most integral for team effectiveness and that underpinned all the other dynamics. Without it, the other dynamics were seen as 'insufficient.'

A useful definition of psychological safety

When I (Sue) was writing an academic paper, my draft reader scribbled in red pen around the word 'Interestingly' and wrote a comment saying, 'Interestingly, to whom? This does not seem interesting to me!' When I saw this comment, I felt shame and embarrassment. Perhaps this person was right and what I had written was not interesting at all. I immediately deleted the word and rewrote the sentence. But since then, even though it is over a decade later, whenever I add a word such as 'interestingly' or 'useful' into a sentence (such as in the title of this section), I have a momentary pause as I fear that whoever will read it might judge me in the same way. In this case, I am fearful and uncertain at suggesting that a point that I am making in my writing could be interesting as I am worried about the potential interpersonal cost of doing this – that I may be humiliated or judged.

So, many definitions of psychological safety focus on the concept of interpersonal risk taking, and a psychologically safe environment being one in which people can speak up with even 'half-baked' ideas, questions and concerns, and disagree with one another or own their mistakes, without fear or punishment or humiliation (Edmondson 2018). On our podcast[1], we talked to Tom Geraghty (founder of Psych Safety)[2] and Stephen 'Shed' Shedletzky (speaker, coach and author) about the definitions that they use the most. Shed told us he recognizes two factors that are essential to enable people to feel able to 'speak up', which are psychological safety and perception of impact, that is, is it safe, and is it worth it? He recognized that there might be times that people push themselves out of their comfort zone and decide to take a risk to speak up, even if a team does not feel particularly safe, when the stakes are really high (such as when someone can see a mistake that could have a profound impact on someone's life). However, experience tells us that, even in these situations, people do not always feel able to speak up.

AN EXAMPLE OF THE IMPACT OF CULTURE ON PSYCHOLOGICAL SAFETY

Ashley[3] first joined the inpatient service as a trainee. She was excited about joining, as she had always wanted to work in a service where there was multidisciplinary team working, and

---

1   https://open.spotify.com/episode/2MzWBiV23Q8eg3i3aMjxJk?si=9SIycs4mQx-Cest2OTwGupg

2   https://psychsafety.co.uk

3   A made-up name, for purposes of anonymity.

it was an opportunity to work closely with a senior lead who was highly respected within their profession. When Ashley arrived, she went through an induction and then spent some time shadowing others on the ward, learning about the rules and expectations of the role. It was eye-opening, as Ashley found the ward fast-paced and quite chaotic at times, with high levels of risk. Ashley found this emotionally difficult and found it hard to switch off when she got home. The senior nurses, including Ashley's supervisor, seemed to take the work in their stride, which Ashley found reassuring and containing. During one of Ashley's first shifts, she noticed something that concerned her. When the 15-minute observations chart was handed over to her, there were quite a few boxes empty (which would suggest that the previous nurse had not completed the observations fully during their shift – implying that they had not 'checked in' with each person on the unit to see if they were safe). When Ashley queried this, the other person laughed and said that this happened all the time, that these were often missed as the staff were just so busy, and that she'd get used to it soon. This made Ashley feel uncomfortable at first, as it felt wrong, as surely these were important checks. But it seemed that management were aware of what was happening, as 'everyone did it'.

She wondered whether to raise this with her supervisor, but it seemed as if her supervisor was already aware and was not doing anything about it. It didn't feel safe to raise it with senior management, as Ashley didn't want to be seen as a troublemaker and risk the fallout from her colleagues, who would likely be angry at her for raising this. It also made her question whether it would be seen that she just didn't understand the ways that things were done and could appear stupid and naive. Perhaps this was how things happened in all similar units. If it really was that bad, surely the senior lead, whom she respected, would have said or done something about it. Ashley later found out that when these checks were missed, the next person filled in the forms as if all the checks had been completed, backdating the signatures and times. At first Ashley avoided doing this, but then as the pressures and chaos of the ward and paperwork ramped up, she, too, started to do this.

Years later Ashley was supporting new staff inductions on the ward. When a new member of staff queried why some of the observations had been missed, Ashley glanced over to a colleague and stifled a laugh, and explained that there wasn't always time to complete them all, but that was just the way that things were done.

What we mean by interpersonal risks

Interpersonal risk is the fear that other people will perceive us in a negative way, which can lead to rejection, humiliation or shame. Sometimes the cost of this can feel particularly high, and immediate – for example, when someone shares a suggestion or idea, and they see another member of the team smirk, say something under their breath or roll their eyes. Even when you have people in your team who are extremely knowledgeable and experienced, they may choose not to share their perspectives for fear of upsetting others, getting things wrong or standing out. People may be fearful of conflict and try to avoid it at all costs. They may fear looking 'stupid', ignorant or incompetent, and others judging them, so we may see them nodding along and seeming to know what they are doing (even if they do not). This may also make them less likely to admit if they have made any mistakes or errors. If people have been dismissed or their ideas ignored or rejected previously, they may be fearful of suggesting things or raising concerns.

People can understandably often choose to hold back rather than speak up, as it feels safer. So, when we are asking people to speak up, we are asking them to step out of a comfortable position (where they can hide in the background and minimize interpersonal risks) to a place where they are facing potential interpersonal risks head on. This can then lead people to avoid discussing or addressing challenges head on, and instead pretending that everything is fine. Underneath this, their resentment and frustration may be building up, which is likely to then play out in other, interpersonally damaging, ways.

Another important point is making sure that sharing your perspectives or ideas is 'worth it'. There may be times when people are encouraged to share their view or perspective, but when they do, it does not feel that it is fully listened to by the leader or acted on. For example, a new leader might come into an organization communicating their interest in hearing the employees' opinions and putting some 'listening exercises' in place to ensure that there is the opportunity for this to happen; however, the same leader might also be closing down conversations, making excuses rather than truly listening (e.g., 'Yes, but we've already done this...'), not appearing to take on board what the employees are saying when considering future planning. This is likely to lead (at least some) staff to feel that this was a tokenistic, tick-box exercise and therefore 'why would they bother' to engage in sharing their views in the future if they were not going to be taken seriously. Sadly, we see this happening a lot within organizations, which can lead to staff feeling dejected and unvalued, leaders losing the trust and respect of their teams, and important communication, concerns and views not being expressed or acted on. It is useful to recognize that the higher up you are within an organization, the less likely you are to know about what is really happening in day-to-day practice.

However, this does not mean that all suggestions and concerns need to be acted on all the time. The reality is that there may be times when it is not appropriate to act on a suggestion that is put forward, or perhaps there are lots of different suggestions that will require prioritizing. As a leader we should be clear when we are opening things up for collaboration, when we are wanting to think things through with the team, and when decisions have already been made within senior leadership. Not everything will need to be brought to our staff for consultation. When we are taking a particular decision forward, and not others that have been proposed, it is important that we let people know that we value that they have chosen to speak up and share their views. We should confirm that we are interested in their opinions, and give some context and the rationale for why we have made the decision we have. This will then make it far more likely that they will feel more able to share their perspective again in the future. Just as important as this direct experience, other members of the team will also witness this exchange of ideas and perspectives. Our responses as a leader will also influence how safe they feel with us to share their views, and thus how likely they are to do so. Therefore, our responses influence the psychological safety within the direct relationship with our colleague and also the sense of safety in the larger team. If we are seen to thank someone for their contribution, and appear to take it seriously, our colleagues will be far more likely to speak up and contribute.

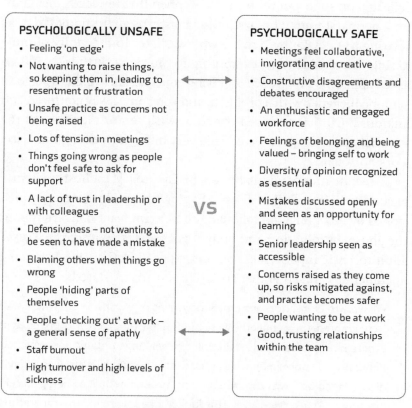

PSYCHOLOGICALLY UNSAFE

- Feeling 'on edge'
- Not wanting to raise things, so keeping them in, leading to resentment or frustration
- Unsafe practice as concerns not being raised
- Lots of tension in meetings
- Things going wrong as people don't feel safe to ask for support
- A lack of trust in leadership or with colleagues
- Defensiveness – not wanting to be seen to have made a mistake
- Blaming others when things go wrong
- People 'hiding' parts of themselves
- People 'checking out' at work – a general sense of apathy
- Staff burnout
- High turnover and high levels of sickness

VS

PSYCHOLOGICALLY SAFE

- Meetings feel collaborative, invigorating and creative
- Constructive disagreements and debates encouraged
- An enthusiastic and engaged workforce
- Feelings of belonging and being valued – bringing self to work
- Diversity of opinion recognized as essential
- Mistakes discussed openly and seen as an opportunity for learning
- Senior leadership seen as accessible
- Concerns raised as they come up, so risks mitigated against, and practice becomes safer
- People wanting to be at work
- Good, trusting relationships within the team

Psychological unsafety vs safety

When our team has good psychological safety, it can feel much more comfortable to share half-baked ideas, as there is less chance of inter-personal harm. In such teams, sharing ideas, even half-baked, is seen as a positive thing to do, and the act of sharing will not negatively impact the reputation of the person or their relationships with others in the team. Unfinished ideas can be an important part of creativity and innovation.

Serious concerns, whistleblowing and speaking up

Sadly, we often hear concerning stories of staff feeling victimized following their speaking up about practice concerns. In an article that we wrote for *HR Magazine* (Knowles and I'Anson 2023), we reflected on some quotes from Dr Stephen Brearey, lead consultant on a neonatal unit, who first raised concerns about potential risks relating to Lucy Letby, a nurse who was later found guilty of mur-dering seven babies and attempting to murder a further six. When asked about his experience of raising concerns, he stated, 'You go to senior colleagues with a problem, and you come away confused and anxious... Clinicians raised concerns with senior members of the hospital and their lives were made very difficult by doing that' (see, Cursino 2023).

A recent independent review of Greater Manchester Mental Health NHS Foundation Trust (Shanley 2024), which was commis-sioned by NHS England following some significant concerns about the abuse, humiliation and bullying of patients within the Trust's adult forensic inpatient service (as exposed in the BBC *Panorama* documentary in September 2022 (Plomin 2022)), stated:

> We were told of various examples, occurring over many years, where staff were ignored, their concerns were minimized, they were reprimanded or experienced professional retaliation for speaking up about poor practice. Reporting of concerns (such as unsafe nurse staffing levels) was actively discouraged and was described by numerous people as being 'career limiting'... At a service level, this looked like low reporting for staffing and 'no harm' incidents. At the most senior levels of the organization,

this looked like pressure to present performance in an opaque, vague, and unduly positive light. (Shanley 2024, p.44)

This last comment highlights not only the lack of psychological safety for the people working within the service, but also the lack of safety and the big pressures that the senior leadership felt to present how the service was performing in a positive way. Where this is part of the culture of the organization, leaders may also fall into these patterns of feeling it is unsafe to speak up themselves, which can lead to the silencing or avoidance of those raising concerns. Clearly this culture and behaviour can result in serious incidents and is an example of *avoidable failure*, as discussed in Chapter 2.

SELF-REFLECTION

- Think about a situation at work where you have not felt psychologically safe. What was happening? How did you feel? How did you react?

- Think about a situation at work where you have felt quite psychologically safe. What was happening? How did you feel? How did you react?

Psychologists and psychological safety

You might assume that psychologists would be absolute experts at psychological safety – I mean, it's in the name! However, there is something about our role and training, and often our personalities, that can make it hard for us to feel psychologically safe and able to speak up. We are trained to be highly attuned (to the person we are talking to, to others in the room, to any underlying dynamics that might be at play), empathic (feeling *with* others), and to have a great awareness of how what is said may 'land' (impact the other person, their underlying thoughts or feelings). We then adapt our language and non-verbal communication accordingly. We are also trained to be good listeners, and to really hear and validate the experiences and perspectives of others.

Therefore, in our experience, psychologists can often be fearful of sharing their own perspectives or views within a group or bringing disagreement or challenge for fear of upsetting others. This includes causing conflict, knowing the impact of what they say may have on another person, or believing that it is their role to bring harmony and 'manage difficult interpersonal dynamics' rather than cause them. Furthermore, when this is their modus operandi they might be upset and angry with others who think differently and value speaking up, even when it causes discomfort and has personal risk attached. This can make it even more difficult for those individuals to speak up, to feel heard and valued, which can lead to an echo chamber within the profession or the polarizing of people and positions, as individuals feel defensive, attacked and angry. This is an example of how a narrowing of opinions and a lack of psychological safety can occur in our profession, but we have observed that the same can also happen in many other caring professions, and within our society on a larger scale.

We have discussed this as a team and have acknowledged that it is important that we disagree sometimes and can have debates around really sensitive and difficult subjects that affect our profession and our work, so that we are not just an echo chamber. We have acknowledged that it is quite normal for teams to have struggles with one another at times, and that is okay, and we can work through them and repair where needed. This is perhaps something to be mindful of within the health, social care and education sectors. Is there something unsaid that is preventing people from feeling safe to challenge or express their views openly?

Our emotional backpacks

Within your team, everyone will bring different experiences from their personal lives and their work. They will have stories of their work within different teams and with different leaders, with differing experiences of psychological safety, or a lack of it, within a work context. We know that our experiences (both personal and work-related) from early life onwards impact greatly on our sense of ourselves and others. It affects how we expect others to behave towards us, and our feelings of trust (see Chapter 7 for more information). One way to think about this is to consider our 'emotional backpacks' and what we might carry with us day to day, which will impact how we 'show up' in our current team. Tom Geraghty described this within our generating safety podcast,[4] where he talked about how our historical experiences within work can impact how safe we feel within our current team.

For example, if we spent several years within a team where there was a culture of silence, where everyone pretended that everything was okay, when people who attempted to raise concerns were silenced or ignored, the result would likely be that when we go into our next workplace, we would still not feel confident to raise any concerns or share a perspective as we would assume that the same would happen again. Furthermore, if we have worked within an organization where a punitive or dismissive response has been dished out to those raising concerns, we may be intensely fearful of sharing anything that could be viewed as critical. This fear can stay with us, and we may find it difficult to 'lose the backpack' of previous experience, even if we are now surrounded by a safe culture and team.

This can make it particularly difficult for a leader who joins a team who have previously experienced a culture where it is unsafe to speak up. The new leader would then need to bring about a real culture change to enable their team to feel safe to share, which is a significant task.

In our Leadership Training, we also explore many of the different factors that can impact psychological safety at an individual, team, organizational, professional, systemic and societal level. An awareness of the different factors that may foster or reduce the psychological safety within your team, and for individuals, can lead to deeper discussions and understandings of what can prevent people

---

4   See https://podcasters.spotify.com/pod/show/evolvingleads/episodes/
    Generating-Safety-e23u77h

from contributing or enable them to contribute their opinions and raising concerns or challenges. Talking this through and working together to identify potential enabling or disabling factors can also be a useful exercise to do with your team.

The importance of psychological safety in health, social care and education

In addition to all these positive outcomes, there are other layers in which psychological safety is needed within the health, social care and education sectors. In these sectors, staff often need to work closely together (interdependent working) to ensure a client's/patient's/student's safety and wellbeing. This can include lots of quick, on-the-spot decision making, where it is important to know that the people around you are going to support you and will tell you if they think that you are making a mistake or getting something wrong. When there are high levels of risk involved, psychological safety within a team can support the group to be thoughtful and reflective, to bring all views and debates to the table, and to make collective decisions where everyone is on board. It is important for people to be able to share with colleagues when they are unsure about a decision or want some more advice, and to check and challenge colleagues and even individuals in more senior positions. When you know that the people around you will talk openly, honestly and frankly, and share any ideas or concerns, it can feel much safer to be able to take a positive risk or make a clear decision. Additionally, these roles are often full of pressure and stress, so it is also important for staff to feel able to share how they are feeling and managing, and to ask for support where needed.

Furthermore, when working in these settings, there may be several relational and organizational dynamics that play out due to the high level of risk, stress or trauma within the work (see Chapter 4), and it is important for teams to feel safe enough to acknowledge when these are happening, to speak up, and to work through challenges as they occur. If these dynamics and associated challenges are not discussed, and remain unchecked, there is a danger that they will continue to permeate the culture of the service or organization, leading to traumatized, stuck and rigid systems that can hinder or even retraumatize, rather than help, the people they are aiming to support.

Candour for personal leadership growth

It is also important, for us as individual leaders, to be able to seek out and receive frank, honest feedback from those around us. Although it can be comforting to receive many positive comments and praise (which may lead to some leaders surrounding themselves with people who treat them in this way), it's also important to have people with whom we work closely who will give us honest, and sometimes challenging, feedback (but hopefully in a kind manner). This helps us to build a greater self-awareness (including how others perceive us and our actions), to know when we are doing things that might be unhelpful, and to keep us grounded. It also means that we can trust that those close to us will let us know when we get things wrong or need to change our approach. When we get honest feedback from those close to us, it is important that we listen to it, and thank the person for letting us know their view. This will encourage them to be able to bring challenge to us again.

A false sense of safety

In some environments it might appear that there is good psychologically safety, but there may be deep cracks underneath the exterior. Sometimes people within organizations feel discouraged about raising concerns or talking about the challenges within the system. They may feel that the organization (or senior leadership) does not want to hear anything that is not entirely positive. We recently visited such a service, where, on the surface, everyone seemed content, happy and positive about the organization. It seemed like a great place to work. However, once we were able to speak to people individually, they started to warn us about some of the challenges that they were facing, and spoke about their unhappiness with some things that were happening. They said that their concerns were often ignored or discounted, for the 'good of the clients'. They believed in the ethos of the organization, but felt that it did not always live up to its values, especially towards staff. When they tried to raise issues, they did not feel heard, and excuses were made. This made it difficult for them to challenge things further, so staff tended to 'get on with things', or eventually leave. This is often referred to as the 'watermelon effect', where on the outside everything appears green, and the team seems to be happy and performing well. However, if you were to break apart the watermelon, you would quickly see the red flesh, indicating that there may be serious hidden problems underneath (ABB 2017).

Therefore, when we see teams that seem to be working well together *all* the time, and are highly positive, with *no* issues or challenges, and *never* any conflict, there is a likelihood that the team are, in fact, lacking psychological safety and are needing to 'mask' normal team issues. Amy Edmondson undertook research in the mid-1990s (see Edmonson 1999) regarding the factors of an effective team in a healthcare setting. She was part of an interdisciplinary research team that was focusing on medication errors in hospitals. They collated data around errors over a six-month period, while also observing and trying to understand how the different medical units worked, their team culture and their behaviours. Amy understandably assumed that the teams who worked most effectively together would make the least number of errors. The research did find a big difference in error rates across the teams. However, something strange arose in the data – the teams that appeared to be the 'better' teams (in terms of feeling mutually respected, more satisfaction in their roles, greater collaboration, etc.) appeared to be making more errors than the teams that appeared to be less effective overall. This would suggest that the most effective teams made more mistakes. This did not seem to make sense. From this conundrum came a new understanding – perhaps the teams who work most effectively do not make more errors but have a culture where it is acceptable to discuss and talk through mistakes that have been made to learn from them. This would inevitably lead to a higher number of reported mistakes. When this was explored further by a researcher who was 'blind' to the initial findings, they found that the teams that worked together most effectively had a culture where they could talk openly and honestly about errors. They used this as a learning opportunity to prevent future errors occurring, whereas those who work less effectively were less likely to feel safe enough to talk about and reflect on mistakes.

Psychological safety: a team responsibility

As Edmondson (2018, p.16) states, 'Psychological safety is about candour and willingness to engage in productive conflict so as to learn from different points of view.' Although this chapter focuses primarily on the building of psychological safety from the perspective of a leader (as leaders have such a large influence on the perception of safety within the team), a leader cannot create psychological safety alone. There needs to be a team commitment to working this way, with courage to be able to speak up, social sensitivity to our roles within the group and a willingness to disagree with respect. Members of the team need to be aware of the impact that they can individually have on the felt psychological safety of others. This can take a degree of self-awareness and noticing of behaviours, for example, talking over others or taking over a discussion, stepping back and choosing not to share an opinion (even if they feel strongly about something), a lack of curiosity or presenting definitive views when it may be unhelpful to do so. It is important to notice any power dynamics that might play out, such as the impact of hierarchy and whether the safety of discussions (and what is shared) changes when particular individuals enter or leave the room.

There are also several non-verbal behaviours that can reduce the sense of safety. Commonly cited behaviours that can be damaging to interpersonal safety are stifled giggles, people looking at their phones, cameras being turned off on video calls, whispers and eye rolling. However, more positive non-verbal behaviours can also be used to help people to feel safer, such as encouraging eye contact, open bodily posture and jotting down notes/writing things out together. Similarly, inviting people into conversations, or asking their views and modelling the sharing of alternative/different views, can be a helpful way for team members to start to create a culture where all perspectives feel valued.

It can be useful to get a measure of the perceived psychological safety in your team. On Amy Edmondson's Fearless Organization website,[5] there is free access to a seven-item measure that assesses psychological safety within a specific team. The survey asks responders to consider how members of the team respond to

- people making mistakes,

- whether people are able to share any problems or issues that they are facing,

- whether people are accepted with their difference,

- whether it feels safe to take a risk,

- how able people feel to ask others for help,

- whether people feel that others in the team are likely to undermine their efforts, and

- whether individuals feel that their particular skills and talents are valued by team members.

SELF-REFLECTION

- Thinking through the list of psychological safety questions above which do you think would be strengths for your team, and why?

- Which do you think will be potential areas for development, and why?

5   For a free personal psychological safety survey, see https://fearlessorganizations can.com

TEAM TASK: EXPLORING PERCEPTIONS
OF PSYCHOLOGICAL SAFETY

It can also be useful to discuss these questions with your team or ask them to rate the questions anonymously (then share the overall findings with the team, to consider what might have shaped their responses). This can help to start to build a greater understanding of what might be impacting on felt safety within the team, and help you (and the team) to create a plan to address this and enhance team safety.

TOP TIPS FOR HOW TO BUILD PSYCHOLOGICAL SAFETY
So far in this chapter we have outlined the importance of psychological safety and reflected on some of the inherent challenges. We have recognized that although the leader has an essential role in creating a culture of psychological safety, it is also a shared responsibility within a team or service. Here we suggest some ways in which you, as a leader, can build and enhance psychological safety within your team or organization.

• *Talk about it and make it part of your team or organizational culture.* Encourage and set expectations around psychological safety. Talk about why it's important, and reflect with your team to get their understanding of why it might be particularly important in your team (with the specific context in which you work). Talk about what it might look like (and what it doesn't look like). Ensure that the team know that they all play a part in how psychologically safe the team is, so that it is a shared responsibility across the team. Ask the team about how psychologically safe they feel, and ask about things that might affect their feelings of safety (refer back to the psychological safety questions), and regularly check in about this.

It can be useful to be explicit at times about how you

want people to be open within a particular discussion. For example:

I am aware that within our senior leadership team, we can sometimes prioritize getting on with each other and being 'kind' over bringing challenge. Can I ask that in the meeting today, while we discuss something of particular importance, we put this to one side and create a discussion where it is okay for anything to be said without causing offence? Where we trust fully in the good intentions of each other to raise what we feel is right for the overall organization? This will help us to have frank discussions. I am happy with whatever outcome we decide on, as long as I can feel confident that you are all behind the decision that we have agreed and have not held back any concerns.

- *Acknowledge (say thank you) when you see someone speaking up, asking questions or raising concerns.* Show the team how you respond positively, and show encouragement and enthusiasm when someone does this. As we know that there is an interpersonal cost to speaking up, we want to make sure that people in the team can see that it is valued and respected by the leader. This can start to create a powerful cultural narrative that 'we want you to speak up'.

- *However, be careful about what behaviour you reward.* Although we want to encourage people to speak up and share suggestions, concerns and ideas, this is not just an opportunity for people to moan or offer excuses for not doing things. When people bring concerns, try to think about how these can be addressed, and attempt to problem solve together. It is also essential to ensure that people remain compassionate towards each other, and do not see this as an opportunity to 'speak up' and criticize other people within the team. As Stephen (Shed) Shedletzky states in his book *Speak Up Culture* (2023), we want to encourage people to discuss and critique ideas rather than people.

- *Understand what the team needs (as a whole and as individuals) to feel psychologically safe.* This can include thinking with the team (refer to the team task) about what might be the barriers to feeling safe, and what they might need to feel more confident to speak up. If you notice particular individuals not contributing much, have a separate conversation with them. This can encourage them to recognize how valued their contribution would be to you as the leader, and to the team, and consider with them what would help them to contribute more (and any barriers to doing this).

- *Find out individual differences in how people want to be rewarded or acknowledged.* Some people might like public praise, but others might find this uncomfortable (and it could even discourage them from speaking up again). Some people might prefer a little note to be left on their desk, or a verbal acknowledgement the next time you meet.

- *Invite people to give an opinion/share a perspective.* Bring people into a discussion, specifically asking for their view or opinion on a matter, and showing that you value their perspective. You can do this during a meeting where it feels appropriate, or you may decide initially (particularly with people who are more hesitant) to give them prior notice beforehand (e.g., 'In this meeting later, we're going to be discussing X... I would really appreciate it you could share any thoughts that you might have') or check in after the meeting (e.g., 'I noticed that you were quiet in the meeting earlier, but I would really appreciate your opinion on what we were discussing. Could we have a chat about it?... That's an interesting perspective, could you share it with the group next time?'). It can also be helpful to ask people, 'What could I be missing?' when having discussions within a group, to show that you want other or alternative views.

- *Try to encourage everyone to speak up.* Be mindful that

naturally within a group there might be one or two individually who will dominate conversations, particularly if
they feel passionate about a subject, are more confident
or feel a sense of responsibility to answer when a question
is asked. Despite good intentions, this can then make it
more difficult for others to share their views, as they may
fear being dismissed or talked over. Therefore, one of your
roles as the leader is to help to manage this. This could
be by acknowledging and thanking the people who have
contributed, but then perhaps asking what views other
people have that differ from those expressed already, or
that might offer a different perspective or opinion.

- *Give a rationale when you do not take a suggestion or obser-
  vation forward.* Encouraging psychological safety does not
  mean that as a leader you have to agree with everything
  or take on every suggestion or idea. But when you decide
  not to, it is still important that the person knows that their
  idea has been heard and considered. It is important to let
  the person know why you have decided not to take their
  idea forward on this occasion.

- *Show some vulnerability as a leader.* Ask for help, acknowledge when you don't know or don't have all the answers,
  or when you have made a mistake. Model the behaviour
  that you want to see from the rest of the team, and this
  will show others that they can do the same.

- *Be curious.* When people challenge your views, or offer a
  different opinion, be aware of any urges to shut them down
  (we all have these urges sometimes, and we might be more
  vulnerable to them when we are feeling under pressure or
  in a rush to make a decision). Instead, try to be curious, and
  ask for their ideas or opinions. You never know what you
  will learn, or how it might shape your perspective.

- *Take turns in leading meetings.* Encourage different team
  members to take a turn leading meetings, allowing you,

as the leader, to be a participant, and therefore redressing the inherent power dynamics. It can also be useful to think about how the room is laid out, where people will be sitting, and what that can represent. Change the seating arrangements as needed.

- *Bring playfulness and light-heartedness to discussions as appropriate.* Create a milieu that can feel informal and creative, with opportunities for collaboration and encouraging people not to take themselves too seriously. From a neuropsychological perspective, being genuinely playful and having fun can create a rush of neurochemicals that increases feelings of trust, bonding and safety and reduces feelings of fear or mistrust (which can prevent us from communicating well, collaborating or learning).

- *Build a culture where learning reviews are embedded as opportunities for learning and improvement.* As the leader, try to avoid focusing on blame, or who did what, as we know that this can lead to feelings of shame, conflict and defensive practice that shuts down our ability to work collaboratively or learn. Instead, use them as a learning and exploration exercise, where the team can think together about what went well, what went wrong and how things could be improved/adapted in the future. In these discussions, it can be useful to think from a position of collective responsibility (e.g., how can we...) rather than focusing on an individual (e.g., how can you...).

- *Create the opportunity for debates as a way of helping staff to practise sharing differing views and arguments.* This could even take the form of a debating club, with topics that have nothing to do with your area of work – perhaps encouraging staff to support an argument that is at odds with their current point of view. This can help to enhance curiosity and the widening of thinking, as well as creating healthy disagreements and debates. To start the gathering of different opinions, you might want to ask people to rate their confidence regarding their argument on a scale of 0–5 (where 0 is 'not at all confident' and 5 is 'fully confident', in their view), and to be curious about what has led to the different scores.

- *Create a team agreement or set of expectations* that is like a social contract drawn up by the team, with a set of clear expectations and behaviours to which they agree to hold themselves, and each other, accountable. This can be a way of saying, 'this is the way that we work here', 'these are our responsibilities to one another' and 'this is what to expect, and what will be expected of you'. This agreement should include thinking about what team members need (from each other and the leaders) to feel safe to speak up, and how any challenges to this will be addressed. It should recognize the role and responsibility of each member of the team in creating a safe environment. It is likely that the agreement will need to adapt and change over time, as the team learns, makes mistakes, and then recontracts around this (see the CMCAFS team charter below). The team agreements tend to be more powerful when they are drawn up by the individual team, bringing context and greater understanding. The act of drawing up the agreement can in itself be an exercise in exploring, challenging and building psychological safety for the team. Where an agreement is created, it is important that it continues to be revisited on a regular basis, so that it is an active discussion, rather than a tick-box exercise. When a 'good enough' version is created, you might want to print it out and have it visible for the team to use. The following is an example of a team charter that we have developed within our team at CMCAFS.

THE CMCAFS TEAM CHARTER: A TEAM AGREEMENT

This is about how we work together as a team. It is not an exhaustive list, and we acknowledge that it can evolve over time, as we grow as a team. We also recognize that this will influence how we work with others.

- We trust in the good intentions of others in the team – they might have a different perspective, but there is a good intent underneath it.

- We try to create a safe space for disagreement, rather than from disagreement.

- We recognize that there may be many different perspectives or stories, and that things are rarely black/white, right/wrong.

- We recognize that toxic positivity is not desirable and expect some difficult discussions and discomfort at times as healthy and normal.

- We find ways to try to hear every voice, recognizing that people might want to contribute to discussions in different ways.

- We are mindful of making sure that there is balance in our discussions, and that we do not just get to hear the fiercest voices.

- We have a 'rant' button, which we can playfully use if we notice that we, or others, are having a solo discussion and taking over.

- We give permission and actively encourage each other to bring different perspectives and opinions. It is acceptable to take a position on something and to disagree with each other. We want to avoid becoming an 'echo chamber'.

- We come from a place of acknowledging that we are all

learning and might get things wrong. We try to take a non-judgemental stance to create an environment where it is safe to make mistakes.

- We encourage 'fierce curiosity' – if there is a view or perspective that we don't understand, we bring openness and curiosity to explore this further and to widen our understanding of the context.

- We try to hold empathy for all of us in these discussions. We recognize that it can take courage and bravery to have these discussions.

- We agree that it is okay to use 'clunky language' to express ourselves, while being open to feedback.

- We try to stay mindful of the language we use and avoid using too many acronyms, to ensure that everyone can stay involved in the conversation.

- Although we might not be connected to a point that someone has made, we try to always stay connected to them as a person.

- We encourage and are open to challenge and recognize the importance of holding a critical perspective (as this helps us to develop). But this should be done in a respectful, kind way.

- We make attempts to include voices that are not represented and to be mindful about stereotyping when 'holding space for others'.

- We try not to take ourselves too seriously, and try to recognize when conversations are getting tough – but we may need to take a break and reconnect, and we are open to repair where needed.

Summary

Throughout the earlier chapters, we have considered how you, as a leader, can enable and empower others, build feelings of trust, recognize, understand and manage relational dynamics, communicate effectively and empathically, and show appropriate vulnerability, which are all key elements to support the building of deep psychological safety within your team. This is a crucial part of being a psychologically responsive leader. It is worth taking the time to consider the sense of safety in your team and what might enhance this for team members. As we have stated, safety does not mean staying comfortable. In fact, it often means tolerating some discomfort while encouraging helpful challenge and debate. Where people do not feel sufficiently safe to speak up, the damage can be devastating to organizations and to those they serve. There are many factors that might impact the sense of safety experienced by an individual, by a team/organization and within a culture. Where we can consider what might be influencing the safety within our team and system, and talk about this openly, this gives us the opportunity to start to address the issues and work together to consider how we can co-create greater safety within the environment. Teams are not safe or unsafe; this is not all or nothing. Safety is dynamic and ever-changing, and is therefore something that the leader needs to constantly consider and support the team to work on.

References and recommended reading

ABB (2017) *Avoiding the 'Watermelon' Effect: Are We Doing Enough in the Process Industry to Prevent the Next Major Accident?* White Paper. https://new.abb.com/uk/media/white-papers

Cursino, M. (2023) 'Lucy Letby: NHS managers must be held to account, doctor says.' BBC News, 22 August. www.bbc.co.uk/news/uk-66578698

Duhigg, C. (2016) 'What Google learned from its quest to build the perfect team.' *New York Times Magazine*, 25 February.

Edmondson, A. C. (1999) 'Psychological safety and learning behavior in work teams.' *Administrative Science Quarterly 44*, 2, 350–383. https://doi.org/10.2307/2666999

Edmondson, A. C. (2018) *The Fearless Organization: Creating Psychological Safety in the Workplace for Learning, Innovation, and Growth.* Hoboken, NJ: John Wiley & Sons.

Geraghty, T. (no date) *Psychological Safety Newsletter.* https://psychsafety.com

Helbig, K. and Norman, M. (2023) *The Psychological Safety Playbook: Lead More Powerfully by Being More Human.* Vancouver, BC: Page Two Press.

Knowles, S. and I'Anson, G. (2023) 'Organisational safety means facing unwelcome truths.' *HR Magazine,* 2 October. www.hrmagazine.co.uk/content/comment/organisational-safety-means-facing-unwelcome-truths

Plomin, J. (Director) (2022, 28 September) 'Undercover Hospital: Patients at Risk.' *Panorama.* BBC

Rozovsky, J. (2015) 'The five key steps to a successful Google team.' Re:Work Blog, 17 November. https://www.michigan.gov/-/media/Project/Websites/mdhhs/Folder4/Folder10/Folder3/Folder110/Folder2/Folder210/Folder1/Folder310/Google-and-Psychological-Safety.pdf?rev=7786b2b9ade041e78828f839eccc8b75

Shanley, O. (2024) *Independent Review of Greater Manchester Mental Health NHS Foundation Trust, Final Report.* Commissioned by NHS England. www.england.nhs.uk/north-west/wp-content/uploads/sites/48/2024/01/Final-Report-Independent-Review-of-GMMH-January-2024.pdf

Shedletzky, S. (2023) *Speak Up Culture: When Leaders Truly Listen, People Step Up.* Vancouver, BC: Page Two Press.

Woolley, A. W., Chabris, C. F., Pentland, A., Hashmi, N. and Malone, T. W. (2010) 'Evidence for a collective intelligence factor in the performance of human groups.' *Science 330,* 6004, 686–688. doi:10.1126/science.1193147.

CHAPTER 10

The EVOLVING Leader: Developing Your Psychologically Responsive Leadership Development Plan

Reading a book such as this can be quite daunting. In each chapter we have included theory, approaches and examples of good practice. As we arrive at the end of the book, we want to reiterate that no leader is fully psychologically responsive, just as no leader is perfect. All leaders will need to keep learning, developing and evolving, adapting to their changing knowledge, experience and context. We hope this book has helped (and will continue to help) you consider each area of leadership practice from a psychological perspective, and therefore enhance your leadership awareness and skills for self-reflection. We hope to help you to continue to gain a wider perspective, build self- and other-awareness, and bring psychologically responsive thinking to your team and organization – the aim of which is to build healthier, more purposeful and productive teams and organizations.

As leaders, when we can build healthier, more purposeful and productive teams and organizations, we can improve both the well-being of the people we work with, through helping them to feel personally connected with the purpose of the work, and a greater sense of pride and achievement in its delivery. By embracing a culture of high care alongside ambitious goals and high standards of practice, we can support our teams to achieve a higher level of performance that serves our clients well, improving their experience of our service and wellbeing, in addition to serving our teams and organizations well.

Our aim is to help you to break down and understand the varying elements of psychologically responsive leadership and team culture that help you to achieve high care, high challenge and high performance so that you can consider how these elements relate to your organization. When you can apply these aspects to your context, and understand that they are continuing processes to be held in mind and worked on, this will be the key to your success.

It may be helpful to share this book and journey with other leaders within your team or with leaders from other organizations who are also interested in developing and improving the culture within their team. This will provide you with someone with whom you can talk things through and learn from how they are applying their learning within their context, or even develop a shared strategy together. Talking through the challenges you experience and strategies to overcome them can be extremely helpful. Many of the leaders who have attended our Leadership Training have told us that having the opportunity to share their experiences, dilemmas, challenges and triumphs with others who understand leadership has been extremely valuable to them.

The psychologically responsive leadership development plan

We have created a draft plan to help you to utilize your reflections, key takeaways from the book and intentions, and to put them into practice (available to download from www.jkp.com/catalogue/book/9781805012368). It is often difficult to put our learning into action when we learn some useful new information, either written or on a training course. It is important to include your personal strengths and resources as a leader that you want to remain aware of and build on, and it is useful to note aspects of your leadership that you feel that you want to develop further, or behaviours or 'pulls' you want to 'catch' to stop yourself falling into unhelpful patterns. You may also make a plan to use some of the activities, information or reflections we have shared with you in the book with your team or organization. It is extremely helpful to take the opportunity to think, reflect and take on new information, and then consider how to use this information in the future, make a plan, and decide how you will hold yourself accountable. This is important to keep your leadership EVOLVING.

We have divided this plan into several sections, which map on to the different chapters within the book, to structure your thinking regarding some of the key aspects of leadership. You will need to consider yourself personally as well as the context of your team and work:

- My motivating factors (Chapter 1)

- Opportunities for creativity and innovation (Chapter 2)

- My 'why' and values (Chapter 3)

- My personal leadership vision and goals (Chapter 3)

- What I need to feel okay (Chapters 4, 5 and 6)

- My strengths and resources as a leader (Chapter 6)

- Areas I want to develop further (Chapter 6)

- My trusted 'inner circle' (who I can go to for feedback, support and advice) (Chapter 7)

- My leadership story (Chapter 8)

- Generating safety (Chapter 9)

- Key reflections and actions.

My motivating factors (Chapter 1)

What helps to keep me feeling motivated and driven as a leader (the factors I currently have, or factors that would help me to feel more motivated and engaged):

. . . .

. . . .

Opportunities for creativity and innovation (Chapter 2)

What opportunities do I have for creativity and innovation within my role, or where could I create opportunities for creativity and innovation within my team?

. . . .

. . . .

My 'why' and values (Chapter 3)

My personal 'why':

. . . .

. . . .

My core values as an individual and as a leader:

. . . .

. . . .

. . . .

How I can move more towards my core values/any intentions I want to set around these:

. . . .

. . . .

. . . .

. . . .

My personal leadership vision and goals (Chapter 3)

(What kind of leader I wish to be – what it will look like if I am fully living my values in a few years' time, and any goals I wish to achieve within my leadership role.

. . . .

. . . .

. . . .

What I need to feel okay (Chapters 4, 5 and 6)

In Chapter 5 we discussed the importance of setting the emotional tone and being an emotionally containing presence for your team. When you are emotionally containing for both individuals and a team of people, it can be exhausting. This is sometimes known as 'collective emotion'. We can experience these emotions quite intensely and can find it hard to stay regulated ourselves. We may end up taking these emotions home with us at the end of the day. It is therefore important to be aware of and manage our own feelings and emotional responses, and those of others. We need to be authentic, but not too open about how distressed or overwhelmed we might be feeling with our team. We need to balance being compassionate and caring, while still driving performance forward. We need to bring calm, encouragement and steadiness, even when we are not feeling it.

Work can become all-consuming when we have such high levels of responsibility with long hours. It can take up a lot of headspace even when we are at home, and everyday self-care can diminish. This is all a lot for leaders to balance and cope with, and there is a danger that without looking after ourselves, we could end up burning out. It is key therefore to consider and prioritize what you need to look after your own wellbeing, and what you might need from others too.

Situations or events (at work or home) that might lead me starting to struggle or feeling burnt out:

....

....

....

What I or others might notice if I am starting to become stressed/ burnt out:

....

....

....

Which relational patterns could I unintentionally fall into (e.g., persecutor, super carer)?

....

....

....

Which behaviours might I start to fall into if I am stressed (e.g., micromanaging, avoidance, sharing too much)?

....

....

....

Which basic self-care strategies might be helpful at these times, even if I won't always feel like doing them (e.g., making sure I am getting a good night's sleep, watching what I eat, exercising, spending time doing things that I enjoy, connecting with those I care about)?

....

....

Any more unhelpful 'coping' behaviours I could fall into (e.g., working too long hours, drinking too much alcohol, avoiding seeing friends)?

. . . .

. . . .

What helps me to switch off at the end of a difficult day/week (e.g., going for a run, watching TV, putting my phone away in a drawer)?

. . . .

. . . .

. . . .

What helps me to feel connected to others (e.g., activities you can do, a call with someone you are close to)?

. . . .

. . . .

My strengths and resources as a leader (Chapter 6)

What are your key strengths as a psychologically responsive leader? Consider which strengths you identify in yourself and your practice, and the feedback that you have received from others (e.g., 360-degree feedback):

. . . .

. . . .

. . . .

. . . .

. . . .

. . . .

. . . .

. . . .

Areas that I want to develop further (Chapter 6)

....

....

....

....

....

....

....

....

....

My trusted 'inner circle' (who I can go to for feedback, support and advice) (Chapter 7)

It can be lonely as a leader. Your role will usually be different from those of your colleagues, and you might be in a different office or space from the rest of the team. You will have different boundaries with your colleagues, and you will hold a greater level of responsibility and accountability. You will also hold information that others are not aware of, and you will be unable to talk to those who you support about their colleagues. It is therefore crucial to identify your support network: people who are alongside you throughout your leadership journey, those you can connect with for support and to check things out (and gain some helpful challenge), and individuals who might be going through similar challenges. It is important that you can feel trust in these relationships, so that you feel safe enough to share openly and reflect with them. It can be helpful to think about what your network looks like now, and what you might ideally want it to look like, so that you reach out and build your network. You might also want to access mentoring, supervision or coaching, where you can share confidentially what you are experiencing in a more open way.

The people currently in my 'inner circle':

. . . .

. . . .

What/who am I missing?

. . . .

. . . .

. . . .

Actions that I can take to stay connected with them, or grow my network:

. . . .

. . . .

My leadership story (Chapter 8)

(See the section "Individual leadership stories" in Chapter 8 for prompt questions – you might want to write or draw this out and add to it over time. It can be useful to talk this through with people close to you, asking them to be curious and share their reflections and wonderings, as a way of deepening your understandings of your journey.

. . . .

. . . .

. . . .

. . . .

. . . .

. . . .

. . . .

Generating safety (Chapter 9)

What helps you to feel safe enough to speak up and share your concerns or half-baked ideas, or ask for support?

. . . .

. . . .

. . . .

What could get in the way of you feeling safe enough to speak up?

. . . .

. . . .

. . . .

How you could you, as a leader, help to create a sense of safety within your team or organization (include any practical steps that you are planning to take)?

. . . .

. . . .

Key reflections

What has stood out or resonated with you after reading the book? Anything that you want to remain aware of going forward?

. . . .

. . . .

. . . .

. . . .

Actions to take forward

How can I keep EVOLVING as a psychologically responsive leader?

The leadership development plan

Goal	Actions	Resources	Criteria for success	Timeline

APPENDIX

Values List

Above and beyond

Accessibility

Accountability

Achievement

Adaptability

Adventurous

Agile and flexible

Altruism

Ambition

Anticipation

Appreciation

Approachability

Assertiveness

Attention to detail

Attentiveness

Availability

Awareness

Balance

Being the best

Belonging

Boldness

Bravery

Brilliance

Calmness

Caring

Challenge

Change

Client-focused

Collaboration

Commitment

Community

Compassion

Competence

Competitive

Confidentiality

Connection

Consistency

Continuous improvement

Contribution

Cooperation

Courage

Creativity

Credibility

Curious and inquisitive

Customer satisfaction

Daring

Dedication

Dependability

Determination

Development

Dignity

Discipline

Discovery

Diversity

Dominance

Down-to-earth

Drive

Duty

Ease of use

Effectiveness

Efficiency

Empathy

Empowering

Endurance

Engagement

Enjoyment and fun

Enthusiasm and passion

Ethical

Excellence

Expertise

Fairness

Family atmosphere

Famous

Fearless

Focus on future

Gratitude

Growth

Happiness

Hard work

Helpful

Honesty

Humility

Impact

Improvement

Innovative

Insightful

Inspiring

Integrity

Knowledge

Learning

Listening

Local

Loyalty

Mastery

Meaning

Mindful

Openness

Originality

Partnership

Passion

Perceptive

Perseverance

Personal growth

Playfulness

Pride

Proactive

Professionalism

Profitability

Quality

Reflection

Relationships

Reliable

Resilience

Respect

Responsiveness

Self-awareness

Skilfulness

Success

Sustainability

Teamwork

Thorough

Toughness

Transparency

Trust

Understanding

Uniqueness

Unity

Useful

Vision

Welcoming

Winning

Wisdom

Work–life balance

Index